Praise for
The Gaslighting of the Millennial Generation

"*The Gaslighting of the Millennial Generation* systematically debunks most of the media's oversimplifying claims about our generation."

—Caroline Beaton, journalist for *Forbes*, *Psychology Today*, and The Huffington Post

"This is a must-read for anyone who wants a better understanding of the betrayal of a generation told they could be anything if they worked hard, only to be mocked and shamed as the American Dream slips further from their grasp. It's time to listen, rather than blame the messengers."

—Melanie Childers, Master Certified Confidence Coach

"So often media outlets throw my generation in my face as the ruiners of life, which makes Caitlin Fisher's book necessary, among other things. Her musings are relatable, her writing style is hilarious, and her unwavering support of Millennials makes me proud to be one. Kudos to her for offering up her personal insights as a connector for so many of us."

—Nina Rossi, founder, Bright Thoughts

T0125844

THE GASLIGHTING OF THE MILLENNIAL GENERATION

THE GASLIGHTING OF THE MILLENNIAL GENERATION

How to Succeed in a Society
That Blames You for
Everything Gone Wrong

CAITLIN FISHER

Mango Publishing
CORAL GABLES

The Gaslighting of the Millennial Generation: How to Succeed in a Society That Blames You for Everything Gone Wrong

Library of Congress Cataloging-in-Publication number: 2019935675
ISBN: (print) 978-1-63353-884-9, (ebook) 978-1-63353-885-6
BISAC category code: SOC022000 SOCIAL SCIENCE / Popular Culture

Printed in the United States of America

To Jess.

You are my hero and my best friend.
I'm sorry about the chalupa.

Table of Contents

Introduction

Or "Who the Hell Are You and Why Should I Read Your Book?"

H ello there! I'm Caitlin Fisher, you probably don't know me, and I'm fed up with everyone saying Millennials are entitled brats. In 2016, I'd been kicking this idea of generational gaslighting around in my head for months, and it finally made it out of my brain and onto my blog. And it turned out that over a million people found that I had finally said the thing they couldn't quite put their finger on. And now it's a book!

Let's be real: It is total bullshit that our generation was raised being told we could do anything but then blamed for everything wrong with society. We're just doing our best, people. Sometimes with three jobs and no health insurance! In my early twenties, I was divorced, living with my parents, on food stamps, with a master's degree and a resume that was getting no bites.

Master's degree. Food stamps. Fifty grand in student debt. This is a real thing that happens. And when we say, "Whoa, you guys told me a master's degree would help with my career and that this was 'good debt!'" they say, "Um, sweetie, why'd you take out loans if you couldn't afford it? This sounds like a you problem."

This book is a new take on self-help. It's not one of those "think positive to find money and true happiness" books. It's more of a guide to untangling the mess in your head and realizing you're not crazy for expecting more out of life or for being disappointed that you seem to be putting in a lot of work for no reward. Each chapter can be taken on its own or read in succession and will end with a recap section with actionable tips and advice you can browse at your leisure.

So that's the short version of why this book is in your hand. Because so many of us are sick of being pointed at and called whiners, so many of us are tired of explaining to our parents that no, really, you can't just go "pound the pavement" to get a job, and so many of us are just plain tired.

I promise you're not crazy.

Also, there are eleven avocado references in this book that I hope you enjoy.

Preview

The Gaslighting of the Millennial Generation

A t a graduate student conference, I first heard the term "Millennial." As in, practices for faculty and staff to best handle this generation of students. I went in having never heard the term and came out feeling defensive against the notion that an entire generation of young adults had to be *handled,* with prevailing knowledge like "Millennials need participation trophies," "Millennials are sheltered," and "Millennials are hard to work with."

Society loves to hate the Millennial Generation (those born between 1980 and 2000), calling us "special snowflakes" and sarcastically referring to us as "social justice warriors," calling us out for being offended by everything and, everybody's favorite, pointing out how very entitled we are.

Here's the secret: We're not.

The negative opinions directed at Millennials are a perfect example of gaslighting, on a societal scale.

A Primer on Gaslighting

Gaslighting is a form of psychological manipulation, making someone question their own sanity or the validity of their experiences through a combination of outright lies, denial of things that have happened, and generally questioning the subject's thought processes. This boils down to the end result of the victim thinking they're wrong or crazy for feeling the way they do. At its core, it's an emotional abuse tactic.

Have you ever gotten into an argument with a parent, boss, or romantic partner about something that upset you, but by the end of the argument, you've become the one apologizing for some wrongdoing? This is often a result of gaslighting. Gaslighters flip it around and become the victim, and your original feelings never get resolved because the conversation always descends into the other person's victimization. Eventually you stop challenging them at all.

Imagine a similar scenario where you are applying for a job, but the job requires a college degree, and you can't pay for a college degree without a job, so you end up taking out massive loans. When you graduate, you can't get a job without experience. So you take a minimum wage job (or three) to make ends meet, often while working for free in a field related to your major to get a foot in the door. You dare to utter something like, "The minimum wage needs to be raised, people can't live like this," only to receive a barrage of crotchety elders yelling at you about how they got a college education working part-time and how it's your fault for taking out the loans in the first place.

I call bullshit.

Busting the Millennial Myth

If Millennials aren't a bunch of spoiled brats with an entitlement mentality who need a trophy just for putting on pants in the morning, what are they?

I've seen Millennials come together to form supportive communities, in ways that some from older generations may have only dreamed of. I know that the young people of years past partied at Woodstock and believed in love and flower power and bellbottoms. Where did they go when we needed them? What happened to the dreams and the love and the bellbottoms?

I see Millennials arranging charity auctions on social media sites, sending a few dollars via PayPal or Venmo to friends in need, donating and sharing fundraising accounts for funeral expenses, medical bills, emergency surgeries for beloved pets, and more.

Speaking of Venmo, it was created by Millennials (Andrew Kortina and Iqram Magdon-Ismail). As were Facebook (Mark Zuckerberg), GoFundMe (Brad Damphousse), Tumblr (David Karp), Pinterest (Ben Silbermann and Evan Sharp), Mashable (Peter Cashmore), Instagram (Mike Krieger and Kevin Systrom), AirBnB (Brian Chesky), Lyft (John Zimmer), Spotify (Daniel Ek), Snapchat (Evan Spiegel and Bobby Murphy), WordPress (Matthew Mullenweg), Tinder (Whitney Wolfe, Alexa Mateen, Sean Rad, Jonathan Badeen, Justin Mateen, Joe Munoz, and Dinesh Moorjani), and Groupon (Andrew Mason).

I see us trading services and goods to help each other out. I see us buying things from work-at-home moms and small businesses rather than supporting large corporate stores. That's not to say that we're the first to do so—indeed, many Gen X and Boomer individuals also shop small and local as a rule. But Millennials have taken the idea and run to the internet with it, making work from home accessible and lucrative across the globe.

Millennials are driven by a need to empower each other and become independent from the status quo. And it's pissing off the establishment something fierce.

Anecdotal evidence is great, but there's also science to back up the whimsical empowerment driving the Millennial Generation. There are some eighty million Millennials, making us the largest cohort in history—and an easy generation to study. The following statistics are pulled from a 2012 report from the US Chamber of Commerce Foundation.[1]

Not only are Millennials the largest demographic, we're also the most diverse. We are 60 percent non-Hispanic white (compared to 70 percent for older generations), 19 percent Hispanic, 14 percent Black, 4 percent Asian, and 3 percent mixed-race. Eleven percent of us are born to an immigrant parent. Additionally, "young people are more tolerant of races and groups than older generations (47 percent vs. 19 percent) with 45 percent agreeing with preferential treatment to improve the position of minorities." So the generation that hears "Why are you kids so offended by everything these days?" is offended because we're sick and tired of seeing minorities vilified and punished by systemic racism.

We stand up for what we believe in, and we're not afraid to call it out. So what are we *doing* with our time and energy?

Millennials are multi-taskers, despite the fact that multi-tasking is actually harmful to the brain and leads to a huge decrease in productivity. But, you know, we have to work all these jobs and get everything done, lest we die penniless in the gutter, eulogized as people who just didn't want it bad enough.

Millennials are engaged and expressive: 75 percent have a social networking profile, 20 percent have posted a video of themselves online, 38 percent have between one and six tattoos, and 23 percent have non-earlobe piercings. The research indicates a trend toward "self-promoting," which some skew to mean that Millennials are self-confident (yay) and self-absorbed (sigh). Others take this data to conclude that Millennials are identifying their passions and making their own path instead of following others' paths for them.

Interestingly (or morbidly), Millennials are the first generation in over a hundred years to have a decrease of their average lifespan. [Insert joke here: Something something working themselves to death].

Millennials have a high graduation rate from high school (72 percent in 2012) and high college enrollment rate (68 percent in 2012). Over half (58 percent) of Millennials who enroll in a four-year college graduate within six years.

Data from the New Strategist Press, a consumer trends resource, shares that in 2013, 34.9 percent of Millennials had a bachelor's degree or higher (compared to 34.6 percent of Gen Xers and 31.1 percent of Baby Boomers). Even without graduating, Millennials and Gen X received more college education than the Boomers (63 percent of Millennials, 62 percent of Gen Xers, and 58 percent of Baby Boomers).[2]

Speaking of college, Millennials have an average of twenty-five thousand dollars in student loans. There is more student loan debt than credit card debt in the United States, and tuition rates are rising faster than inflation. However, enrollment continues to increase.

Millennials Struggle with Mental Health

Many Millennials struggle with mental illness to some degree: anxiety, depression, bipolar disorder, and more. You have to wonder how much of that anxiety comes from being told that wanting a living wage, affordable college, or adequate healthcare means that you're a dependent leech guzzling from the government teat.

The generations before us had a more accessible living wage, tuition cost, and adequate healthcare. But now, inflation has reduced the value of the minimum wage, college tuition and loan interest rates are through the proverbial roof, and medical bills are the top cause of bankruptcy in America.

These things were not caused by Millennials, but after a steady diet of hearing "You're entitled" as we developed our adult identities, we don't even need to hear it from other people now. We believe it about ourselves. As a society, we now romanticize struggle, busy-ness, and "the hustle." If you're not losing sleep and working two or three jobs, you must not want it enough.

Conclusions (For Now)

Millennials have begun waking up to the fact that the ways we were treated as children and as young adults in the work force *are not normal.* We're understanding that our generation *is bigger than the last.* We're coming to terms with the fact that we will inherit the earth and want to make it very, very clear that while we absolutely intend to clean up this mess, *we are not the ones that made it.*

Part I

Millennials Are Entitled, Disrespectful Punks

Chapter 1

Millennials Are Killing the American Dream

*"Millennials Say the American Dream
is Dead? They killed it"*

–Red Alert Politics, 2014

*"American dream slips out of reach
for Millennials, study finds"*

–LA Times, 2016

*"Millionaire to Millennials: Lay off the avocado
toast if you want to buy a house"*

–CNN, 2017

The American Dream: having a home, a family with 2.5 kids, a dog, and a white picket fence. The stuff of *Pleasantville* and the '50s and housewives with dinner on the table when dad gets home from work. Maybe it was this way for our grandparents, but the new American Dream is more like having affordable health care, a therapist who takes you seriously, and being able to afford your expenses with only one job. When did the American Dream become a struggle to wake from the slog of reality?

Enter the Millennial troublemakers, screwing things up. We're told that our wasteful and luxurious spending on hipster foods and specialty coffees prevents us from buying a home, but when faced with mountains of student loan debt and spending on necessities like shelter, running water, and medical care, it's hard to find the wiggle room to save up an appropriate down payment. The wiggle room to treat yourself to a latte is much more feasible—and small treats are a normal part of human life, not an opportunity to victim-blame and heap responsibility for the entire economy on a group of young adults who just want a damn cup of coffee between jobs.

On top of a laundry list of skyrocketing living expenses without a comparable wage increase, we see predatory lending schemes that promise young first-time home buyers a zero-percent-down plan with an adjustable rate mortgage. This loan structure is a recipe for economic disaster and another housing crash that will be messier than a smashed avocado. These mortgages are a booming business due to the conventional wisdom that owning is always superior to renting; unfortunately, that's not true at all. Owning a home comes with risks and expenses that renting doesn't, and it's just not wise to purchase a home based on fear and scare tactics from brokers who just want to make a buck before you figure out what they're up to. It's a far better plan to rent affordably while saving up for a modest home, and it has nothing to do with macchiatos.

A note about lattes: Starbucks does charge pretty exorbitant prices compared to a bottomless cup of joe at your average diner. But it's also one of the few employers in the United States to offer comprehensive insurance coverage (medical, dental, and vision) to both full- and part-time employees, as well as a 401(k) with a company match, and a stock equity benefit, in addition to tuition assistance for continuing education and paid vacation time. Starbucks even has a dependent care reimbursement program to help employees pay for day care, life insurance, and disability insurance. But sure, let's get grouchy about the fact that their holiday cups don't have enough Jesus. This is obviously why houses are expensive and the minimum wage is a joke.

Defining the American Dream

The definition of this great dream depends on who you ask. Hearkening back to yesteryear, the American Dream was a promise of a better life in the United States. The tired, the poor, and the huddled masses were promised a new home where anything was possible if you were willing to work hard for it. For as long as there has been a United States of America, there has been a safe refuge for the disenfranchised—at least in theory.

The Merriam-Webster Dictionary defines the American Dream as "a happy way of living that is thought of by many Americans as something that can be achieved by anyone in the US especially by working hard and becoming successful." If we put our minds to it, live within our means, and work hard, we can achieve anything! If this sounds familiar to Millennials, it's because it's the classic refrain of our Boomer parents, who really could hope to achieve their goals with a little elbow grease. Spoiler alert: hard work doesn't really cut it anymore.

Do any other aspects of the American Dream have us ready to face our future with a positive attitude? Why, yes!

The American Dream optimistically involves the desire to improve society for the next generation. It's like camping—leave things in better shape than you found them. For the first several generations of (white) Americans, this was a feasible dream. Many generations have been able to see their children live longer, have better careers and lives, and continue down a path of improvement that first-generation immigrants set out to achieve.

Now it's time for the million-dollar question: are Millennials doing better than their parents? Unfortunately, no. The Millennial Generation is facing shorter lifespans than generations past, in part due to chronic health conditions, drug addiction and overdose, suicide, and alcohol poisoning. This decrease in lifespan also affects the Baby Boomers, though not as starkly. According to Bloomberg's recap of actuarial studies in the US, "the life expectancy for sixty-five-year-olds is now six months shorter than in last year's actuarial study."[3] It turns out that the Boomers, Gen-Xers, and Millennials are all on a downward trend as far as lifespan goes.

Taking Care of Our Own

In the face of declining life expectancies and increased healthcare demand, what's a country to do? Aren't we one of the most developed and prosperous nations in the world? Of course we are, so why are our people dying, chronically ill, and choosing between keeping food on the table and going to the doctor?

The Guardian ran an article online in July 2017, titled, "How Does the US Healthcare System Compare with Other Countries?" which explores just that—how our spending and behavior around healthcare compares with the rest of the world.[4] In one heartbreaking graph, titled "Spending compared with life expectancy," the caption states, "The US was comparable to other developed countries until the early '80s, when healthcare expenditures accelerated and life expectancy rates fell behind." So, not only do we spend more than other countries on our medical care, we're dying sooner too. While other developed countries like Iceland, Australia, Japan, Norway, Switzerland, and the UK show a gradual increase in healthcare spending over time, the US took a sharp turn and is off in outlier la-la land with its fingers in its ears.

The overall health of Americans is on a decline, which is a pretty big deal. As programs like Medicaid and Medicare face government cutbacks, older generations have less access to reliable healthcare. And as insurance prices increase in general, the rest of us may have to choose between maintaining insurance and keeping a roof over our heads.

The decrease in income compared to inflation has drastically moved the goalposts of this great American Dream. While former generations could put in a forty-year career and retire by age sixty-five with the expectation of a comfortable retirement (and even Social Security), the younger generations don't have that same level of expectation. If we can barely pay rent, how are we supposed to save for retirement? Or a home? How can we afford to put our kids in day care while we go to work?

Procreation also brings healthcare expenses and spending on new-baby essentials. Millennials tend to delay parenthood, with research indicating that the average age of a first-time mother in the United States has risen from between twenty-one and twenty-two in 1970 to roughly twenty-six in 2014.[5] There's an obvious correlation to modern feminism and access to contraception, as well as comprehensive sex education. However, there's also the fact that many Millennials just don't have the money for kids until later in their lives. Having a child means time off work, or even leaving the workforce, which can cause a huge financial hit that simply wasn't as big a factor in prior generations. Running a household on a single income in 2019 is possible for a select and privileged few, but certainly not as feasible as it was when our parents were born.

The New American Dream

Some journalists posit that the Millennials' take on the American Dream is a reimagining, while some declare it dead entirely and completely unachievable (whether due to avocado consumption or things like housing costs).

Jason Notte of *The Street* writes, "Millennials have redefined the American Dream" in a May 2017 piece, continuing, "Millennials haven't given up on the American Dream: their expectation of it has evolved."[6] While Millennials still see the classic debt-free retirement with a paid-off house as a staple of the American Dream, they're also adding things like travel and living abroad to their proverbial bucket lists. But, Notte points out, Millennials don't always have the cash on hand to fund their wanderlust.

Millennials definitely enjoy travel, on the whole, and even living in another country for a while. But it appears that they don't tend to stay away for long. Millennials still feel strongly tied to the idea of "settling down" and aren't likely to leave town to move somewhere brand new over and over again. Notte's article gives the following rundown on Millennial moving habits:

"Currently, Millennials only envision themselves packing up and moving to a new city, state or country fewer than two more times in their lives. Most (68 percent) even say they would prefer to build a life in one community, rather than live and work in multiple geographies. At this stage, 43 percent of Millennials have bought their homes, while 75 percent of non-homeowners say they could be motivated to buy a house."

—Jason Notte

We live in an age when it's increasingly easy for young adults to live in another country for months at a time through study-abroad programs at high schools and universities. There are even volunteer organizations that allow you to live in another country for a summer or longer. Friends of mine have spent summers or semesters in Scotland, Ireland, Mexico, and France, and my sister has done a summer volunteer program in Nicaragua and spent a semester in Spain.

Perhaps the ability to so casually leave home and explore other places is a factor of our tech-savvy generational habits. We can Skype, FaceTime, or video chat with our friends and relatives across the globe in an instant, and social media makes it simple to stay in touch no matter where in the world you wander. With such accessible travel and so many places to explore, it's no wonder our younger generations are finding new ways to embrace new cultures and experiences.

The American Dream: Now with 80 Percent More Gaslighting

On a side note, can we take a moment to acknowledge that the American Dream is a perfectly gift-wrapped example of victim-blaming? If your life sucks, it's because you didn't want it enough, didn't hustle enough, didn't do everything in your power to keep up with the Joneses. When the American Dream is out here saying, "I'm so easy to attain if you just try hard enough!" then it's all too easy to heap the blame on the people whose lives are in shambles.

We also need to acknowledge that this belief lets us distance ourselves from people who have it worse. We tend to believe it can never happen to us, because we're focused on the dream and making it happen. But most Americans are one paycheck away from financial ruin, don't have savings, and are trapped in a cycle of debt. And this is *normal* in our society. The American Dream romanticizes living beyond your means while pretending everything is fine. It's toxic denial, and it's time to wake up.

Killing the American Dream

Millennials did not have a big generational board meeting and decide to screw up the idea of owning a home and retiring comfortably. That would be a very silly thing to do, in an attempt to get one over on The Man. Rather, greed has killed the American Dream. Sky-high tuition costs and student loan rates have killed the American Dream. Subprime mortgages have killed the American Dream. The tradition of systemic racism and sexism in America have killed the American Dream. Rising costs and lower wages have killed the American Dream.

And who, might I ask, has left these inequalities in their wake, waiting for us to pick up the pieces? Telling us to be grateful when we rightfully voice the truth? Carpeting over those beautiful hardwood floors? Our parents and grandparents, naturally.

The older generations get annoyed with Millennials because we're forcing and driving change. Baby Boomer landlords, business owners, and bosses now must reevaluate their practices or risk losing business, since Millennials aren't afraid to shop around.

Forbes says, "Employers need to stop blaming Millennial turnover on issues of entitlement, listlessness or impatience and instead look at what these workers want and what they—as companies—have to offer them."[7] Business.com adds, "It's crucial for companies to adjust to [the Millennial] generation to attract and retain talent...Managers need to consider what current and future workers expect from their employers today."[8]

Additionally, services and apps like Whose Your Landlord allows younger renters (i.e., Millennials) to connect with landlords more transparently, seeing reviews from past tenants and getting a true idea of the lodgings available. This startup was developed as more and more young adult renters were falling victim to rental scams and feeling trapped by rent hikes while their chances at home ownership slipped further away.

Whether it's finding a new place to live, a better place to work, or a different brand of chicken nuggets, Millennials vote with their dollars. And it has the Boomers scared as hell.

Making a fuss about how disrespectful and entitled Millennials are derails the conversation and puts us on the defensive. That might have worked when we were kids, but we keep getting older and moving on up the purchasing power ladder. Millennials in their early to mid-thirties are using every penny at their disposal to shape society and hold businesses accountable.

One might even argue that we're changing the American Dream.

How to Make Sure You're Killing It

Know that it's okay to rent. People will tell you that renting is like throwing away money. These people are not in charge of your life. They are also wrong. Renting gives you options. Renting means you have someone who has to fix your broken pipe and the hole in your roof and the furnace. Owning a home may look like a cheaper monthly payment, but when the AC blows in the middle of the summer you are going to realize that you are solely responsible for fixing the broken things and that everything costs money. You can rent your whole life and still achieve happiness. (Plus, the recession and housing bubble burst of 2008 was not a fun time, let's please not rush to buy homes we can't afford.)

Travel, if you want. If you want to travel the world and do cool stuff in other countries or states, plan for it and save up to travel to your heart's content. Plan to sublet furnished apartments to save costs, or travel in hostels or with AirBnB. Travel minimally and consider reducing your possessions to save on keeping things in storage while you are out of the country.

Buy smart. If and when you decide it's time to buy a home, aim to put at least 20 percent down with a mortgage payment no more than 25 percent of your monthly take-home pay (this is the Dave Ramsey recommendation, and he knows what's up). If you make $3,000 a month, your mortgage payment should be $750, give or take. This prevents you from having too much of your monthly income tied up in your housing costs. Also—you may be approved for a loan amount that is much higher than this. That is not the number that matters. The numbers that matter are 20 percent down, and 25 percent of your net monthly income.

Don't fall for zero down. Millennials are at high risk of being targeted for "first-time buyer" schemes that promise an affordable payment and no money down. This is not a safe loan—don't fall for it. While 20 percent is recommended to avoid special insurance called PMI (which adds to your monthly payment), 10 percent down is the minimum you should aim for. You should have zero interest in a zero-down offer.

Invest wisely. Being a Dave Ramsey follower, I recommend you follow his "baby steps" approach to personal finance, which starts with becoming debt-free and saving an emergency fund before starting retirement savings. Your mom may tell you to start saving now to get a head start, but she may actually be more broke than you, with all the cards on the table. If you act smart with your money and get your financial house in order before you start planning for retirement, you should still be well ahead of the game. Invest in quality mutual funds with a good track record, and make sure you understand the nuts and bolts of everything your financial advisor tells you. If they start telling you that you don't need to understand something to put money in it, fire them and try again. You are in charge of your money.

Screw other people's expectations. When your parents and relatives start turning up the "When are you going to settle down?" vibes, feel free to ignore them. You have to do what's going to make your life fulfilled. If that means spending six months living in hostels because you just have to do it before you die, that's cool. Finance your dreams with freelance work you can take with you wherever there's Wi-Fi, or save up a travel fund and spend it frugally.

There's no right time to have kids. It's true that there's never a right time to start a family, but there may be times that are better than others. Evaluate your own financial and family situation to decide for yourself if you're ready to have a child. You might decide to have a baby outside the "norm" of love-marriage-babies by age thirty. You could have a baby before getting married, as a single parent, or even in your forties. You don't have to have all the pieces perfectly in place to get started—you just have to be ready enough. There's also no guarantee it will happen right away, and obviously there are age and health factors that impact fertility, so keep that in mind when you're waiting for the perfect moment to arise.

Be independent. As soon as you can, extricate yourself from your parents' purse strings. When they're supporting you financially, they tend to have lots of opinions about how to run your life. When you can establish a boundary in this area, life changes drastically for the better. They'll still have the same opinions, but you'll feel less obliged to try their opinions on for size. You are the expert on your life.

Chapter 2

Millennials Are Killing Basic Respect

"Why Millennials Annoy Their Elders"

—Forbes, **February 2014**

*"Millennials: A Progressive Generation
with a General Lack of Respect"*

—Odyssey, **February 2017**

The working title of this chapter is "Millennials are Killing Family Values," but I'm not sure it will stay that way. I'll cover a lot of "value"-related ideas in the chapters about relationships and parenting, but "family values" encompasses so much. What it boils down to is that this chapter is all about the way Millennials make their families (usually parents) shake their heads and mutter about what disrespectful kids they raised. Because, of course, the idea that Millennials are entitled and disrespectful jerks needs a foothold, and parents thinking it about their own children locks it in for the rest of society to whine about.

Here's the thing about Millennials. If something or someone treats us badly or makes us feel like crap, we say a hearty "No thanks." This means changing the landscape of the workplace when managers treat us like machines instead of people. This means making a ton of noise about sexual assault and sexism, even though it gets us labeled problematic and routinely told that we're making something out of nothing. This means we'll cut off family members who treat us poorly, and we are unapologetic about it.

From #MeToo, which I'll discuss in more depth later, to the general willingness and empowerment of young people to call out racism, sexism, economic injustice, and other societal issues, we're making a big fuss. And it's changing society for the better, from large-scale protests to tiny battles across the Thanksgiving dinner table. We have no time or space for people who treat other people poorly.

In the last two years of my life, I have made the decision to cease contact with both of my biological parents. When I stopped talking to my mother, she threw all my stuff away and wrote me out of her will. When I stopped talking to my father, he accused me of being the problematic common denominator. And yet, I'm the healthiest and happiest I've ever been, now that I no longer feel responsible for being their version of a good daughter.

Remember this: It's not your job to be what someone else expects of you. You are not obligated to "respect" someone who does not treat you well.

A Little Bit Screwed-Up

If you are anything like me, you got to adulthood a little bit screwed-up by your childhood. I know that no one had a perfect childhood, but it's important to understand that the way your parents speak to you as a child is the way you learn to speak to yourself as an adult.

I believe that the majority of parents love and support their children—but they can still make mistakes in parenting. This is why it's so important to apologize to your kids when you mess up. Acting like you're the authority of all authorities and expecting your children to blindly respect you even when you've hurt them is a recipe for you getting pissed-off when they finally stop talking to you in their thirties. Ungrateful brats.

No matter what issues you have as an adult, they are probably buried somewhere in your childhood. The way we experience life as adults is framed and experienced through the scripts we learned as children. When we are kids, we are absorbing and assimilating new information so fast. There is so much being learned, so constantly, it's a wonder our heads don't explode.

Unfortunately, we also learn coping skills through childhood traumas, and those things tend to stick with you well into adulthood. Sometimes they are beneficial, and sometimes they leave you wondering what is wrong with your damn brain. We grow up with the example of our parents as our barometer of normal, even when outsiders can see that our family is definitely not normal, for better or worse.

Here's a delightful example: Georgia Moffett, daughter of actor Peter Davison (who played the fifth iteration of the Doctor in the British TV show *Doctor Who*), said in an interview, "My father, Peter Davison, played the fifth Doctor. I went to school with the daughter of Colin Baker [the sixth Doctor], so I was sort of under the impression that everyone's dad was Doctor Who."

This is a prime example of how children use their families as the measure of normal against other families. For this same reason, children of abusive parents may continue the cycle of abuse against their own children because they assume that it was normal behavior. Children of healthy families tend to be healthy and respectful in their own parenting practices.

In my case, I never remember seeing or hearing my parents argue, but I felt tension. Then they divorced when I was seven. In my marriages, I never wanted to argue or fight because I had never seen how that was done in a healthy way. I expected that you just lived with the tension until your breaking point, because that was how I witnessed the dissolution of a marriage as a child.

After our parents' divorce, my sister and I moved to Texas to live with our father for a brief stint. I was around twelve years old. I remember telling my dad that I loved him, and he said, "You say that so much that it seems like you are trying to convince yourself of it." I remember feeling like my stomach had been filled with ice, and I had an uncomfortable tightness in my chest. I felt slapped. And with that one offhand statement from a man who was under a lot of emotional strain and vented it at his daughter, I learned that my love cannot be trusted, it must be proven.

Before I figured this childhood issue out, I practically gave myself to death in romantic relationships, never wanting to give the other party reason to doubt my love or think I had to convince myself to love them. I became very easily taken advantage of and taken for granted because of how hard and deep I threw myself into making sure my partner knew I loved them. I never even stopped to notice if that love and attention was being reciprocated.

By the age of twelve, I discovered through constant reminders from my mother that I was fat, lazy, and worthless. My sister and I were put on diets from a young age and were shamed for being hungry, wanting sweets, or going up a pants size. I internalized the message that fat people don't get loved, and I would never find a man to love me because I was fat and lazy: nobody wanted to be with someone like that. The objective of my life became to become pretty and find a man, because I equated that with happiness. So, as an adult, I often went along with whatever a man wanted to do because I didn't want to be rejected.

Moral of the story: I am just as screwed-up as you are.

The bad news is that your childhood is over, and it happened, and you can't go back in time and actually change it. The good news is that you can still work on healing your childhood wounds in order to become a healthier adult. For many, a therapist is helpful in these endeavors, particularly if you were abused by parents or others in childhood, either emotionally, physically, or sexually.

Sometimes, this healing involves cutting your parents or other family members out of your life. And this is one hundred percent okay to do. Even if it makes them angry or they write you out of the will or they say really mean things about you. Even if they say you are a disrespectful child and they don't understand why you don't respect your elders.

Pro tip from me to you: Respect is a two-way street, and you don't owe anybody shit.

The Ways Our Parents Fail Us

I know what you're thinking. How is childhood trauma a Millennial issue? It's not—but we are the ones behind an "epidemic" of family estrangement. According to psychologist Joshua Coleman, "Parenting has changed more in the last forty years than it did in the few centuries before that… The principles of obligation, duty and respect that Baby Boomers and generations before them had for their elders aren't necessarily there anymore."[9] (Shout out to my Gen-X friends who are joining us in this unsavory destruction of society.)

In a post on Bustle, writer Gabrielle Moss shares my difficulty in finding data to support this bubble of estranged Millennials who don't call their parents to gab about their day like besties. She says: "We don't want to raise our voices to say, 'I didn't get told I was special, I was told I was a piece of crap who ruined my mother's life,' because we're afraid to find out that we really are wrong, twisted, different from everyone else."[10]

It's important to note that, while child abuse, neglect, and other traumas are being called out more publicly and freely than in generations past, actual rates of abuse are trending on a major decline. Consider the following excerpt from *Millennials Rising*, published in 2000:

> In this new era of hypersensitivity, people have been alarmed by government reports that child abuse is on the rise. In particular, the 1996 National Center for Child Abuse and Neglect caused a great stir by reporting a huge jump of over 50 percent in the rates of most types of child abuse…between 1986 and 1993. Research by the National Child Abuse and Neglect Data System shows the problem getting sharply worse in the early '90s and then better in the late '90s. All these scenarios are troubling: Is the rate of child abuse really going up?
>
> The answer is: probably not. What the government numbers track is not the actual incidence rate, but the official intervention rate. And in the Millennial child era, experts suspect that rising interventions parallel a rising willingness by neighbors, teachers, nurses, and officers to report possible cases of abuse. As for the trend in actual incidence, the best personal survey data…point in the opposite direction: toward a dramatic decline of over 40 percent in the rate of parental violence against children from 1975 to 1992.[11]

> —Neil Howe and William Strauss,
> Millennials Rising: The Next Great Generation

Millennials are not unique in having experienced traumatic childhoods. But when we are mistreated, abused, neglected, etc.—we talk about it. Hence, I'll be exploring these factors of abuse in my book about Millennials, because we're working to normalize and destigmatize talking about abuse. We're not keeping the family secrets anymore.

Poor parenting has an infinite number of sources and explanations but often takes one of two main tracks in how it is inflicted upon a child: ignoring or engulfing. While there are myriad ways a parent or caregiver may inflict trauma and suffering onto a child, this chapter will deal more with emotional trauma from parents who fail to meet a child's psychological needs for love, approval, affection, and more. The ongoing struggle of children who did not receive emotional support growing up can and will follow them into adulthood and impact their ability to function in the world, in personal and professional relationships, as I mentioned before.

What More Could You Want: The Ignoring Parent

The "ignoring" parent fails to show up for the child's needs. On the most extreme end of this spectrum, there is neglect and abuse: not feeding a child, abusing a child physically or sexually, failing to provide a child with adequate clothing, and so on. In general, the non-extreme variety of ignoring parents tend to their children's physical needs but fail to meet their emotional needs. These emotionally neglectful parents may leave a young child to cry when upset or tell them to get over it or shut up. They may shame or bully their child, overtly favor a sibling over the ignored child, or not pay attention to their child's emotional symptoms like depression or anxiety. The feeling of this parent is something in the neighborhood of, "You have a roof over your head, clothes on your back, and food to eat, so what more could you want?" The answer, of course, is love, support, and attention, which are fundamental building blocks of healthy adult relationships.

The ignored child grows up to be an overachiever, hoping time after time that they'll finally get their parents' attention. Or they grow up to be a self-saboteur, knowing that their efforts have never mattered and will never matter, so why bother? Children of neglectful parents may develop anxiety (how can I do this so I won't mess up or disappoint someone?), depression (what's the point in trying, no one cares), substance abuse problems (I just want to feel something or not feel anything), and eating disorders (I just want to control something in my life).

My own childhood was one with an ignoring parent; my mother just didn't know what to do with emotions. She dropped out of school and left home to live with her grandmother at age fourteen and subsequently grew up very fast. She then expected her children to also act like miniature adults, despite the fact that play and imagination are more developmentally appropriate than scrubbing and re-scrubbing the bathtub. My sister and I grew up feeling like we had to chase Mom's approval through achievement in school and by performing our chores flawlessly. Laziness was the ultimate sin in our house.

From menstruation to sexuality to body image, my mother had no idea how to encourage growth, competence, or confidence. As a twelve-year-old, I asked her if I was fat. She approximated my BMI in her head, ran it through the filter of newspaper articles she had read about obesity in children, and left her response at "Yes." When we had "the talk" about sex, I learned nothing of sexual pleasure or safe sex practices, but I did learn that it was the only thing guys want and that if I "came home pregnant, the only help [she] would offer me is the number to Planned Parenthood." There was no safe space to learn what it means to be a girl or woman beyond "Don't talk with food in your mouth." It was all about image and propriety, never about what we needed emotionally. My childhood was spent aimlessly but thoroughly applying myself toward different projects in the hope that something would make her notice me as a person and not an extension of a mop.

When my physical needs demanded a trip to the doctor to investigate shortness of breath in gym class, I was prescribed an inhaler for exercise-induced asthma. My mother told me it was a fake inhaler the doctor prescribed me as a placebo and I just needed to lose weight. When I asked to go to therapy at age fourteen because I was suicidal, she let me see the open bills on the kitchen counter and did nothing to stop me from feeling guilty over needing care. At the same time, she told me I didn't have depression and there was nothing wrong with me. When I was actually diagnosed with not only anxiety but *severe* anxiety at age twenty-eight, I was shocked. I assumed on some level that I had been faking it or making it up.

Countless friends and acquaintances have had similar experiences with their own parents.

Long story short: when parents act like the needs of their child don't matter, don't exist, or are a burden, it affects the child in fundamental ways into adulthood.

In a 2003 study published in *Child Abuse & Neglect, Volume 27, Issue 11,* researchers investigated whether emotional abuse/neglect are predictors of psychological and somatic symptoms in adulthood. They found that "a history of emotional abuse and neglect was associated with increased anxiety, depression, posttraumatic stress and physical symptoms, as well as lifetime trauma exposure." The conclusion of their study states, "Long-standing behavioral consequences may arise as a result of childhood emotional abuse and neglect, specifically, poorer emotional and physical functioning, and vulnerability to further trauma exposure."[12]

Another study highlighted a connection between childhood abuse/neglect and personality disorders.[13] Specifically, researchers found that emotional abuse was a significant predictor of borderline personality disorder, and all forms of trauma (sexual, physical, and emotional abuse) were predictors of paranoid disorder. Emotional abuse of boys correlated to self-mutilation.

Simply put, an emotionally ignored child is likely to have any number of negative outcomes and maladaptive behaviors as an adult. Children who were raised with emotional abuse face two dangers when raising kids of their own. They may repeat the cycle, having never experienced a healthy example, or they may swing so far in the opposite direction, in an attempt to be different, that they end up stifling their children in a completely different manner with the same result. Of course, it is also possible to learn healthy coping skills and break the cycle.

I'll Never Let Anything Hurt You: The Engulfing Parent

You might think at first glance that being attached at the hip and making sure to be engaged in every aspect of a child's life is indeed more loving, effective, and helpful than being outright neglectful. However, the over-parented child often has similar emotional upheavals and feels just as lonely and ignored. When a parent is there to make every decision, to catch every fall just before it happens, the child never learns to crawl, walk, run on their own. They never have a mistake to learn from. Subsequently, they feel lost and confused when they finally leave the nest.

The engulfing parent may take on the responsibility for the child's social life and activities, which may range from mildly controlling to outright projection of the parent's own unachieved desires, later foisted upon the child whether they want to participate or not. These are the pageant moms, the bequeathers of family businesses, the sports enthusiasts who argue with umpires. Did they ever ask the child what they wanted to explore?

Rebecca reflects on a difficult childhood and an overbearing mother who attended middle school dances and even a job interview with her:

At the time, I didn't know any different. We had just moved from Los Angeles to Eugene, Oregon, and I had only been to private Christian schools. This was my first time going to public school, so having my mom, twin sister, and disabled brother tag along [to the dance] seemed normal. Once I got to high school, I realized it wasn't normal. Neither was my home life.

I don't think I really understood my home life until I started going to public school. I was raised in church and church schools and had a very sheltered childhood. My parents divorced when I was ten and that's when my family moved to Oregon. I'm the youngest of seven and my oldest siblings made it hard to be a teenager. Instead of asking or taking an interest in my life, my mom assumed that I was repeating anything my older siblings had done. I rebelled in high school and was sent back to private school. I moved out when I was sixteen and it took a long time for me to learn to be on my own. My mom always made important calls for me and I still have anxiety over talking on the phone.

My mother going to my first job interview with me was embarrassing. I didn't want her there and I think she answered more questions than I did. Obviously, I didn't get the job.

I even think the way I parent has been affected. I don't want to be my mother, but sometimes I can't let my three-year-old be a three-year-old. When my child plays with things that can make a mess or lead to any possible injury, I stress out and start to hover. My husband has told me more than a few times to just let it go and take a step back. I didn't see my childhood or my mom in a bad way until I moved away from her, and even then it took many years.

This case is more extreme than the typical helicopter case would present, but a surprising number of people in my social circles had similar stories about overbearing parents. Engulfing parents may behave this way because they were ignored as children and want their children to have a better childhood. They may have their own anxieties that cause them to be overprotective or overinvolved. But, to quote Dory from *Finding Nemo*, "You can't never let anything happen to him…then nothing would ever happen to him!"

The over-parented child grows up to be an overachiever, because their childhood was full of activities and it's the only way they know to live. Or they grow up to be a self-saboteur, because they're so tired of having everything planned out and they never want to feel like they are in the spotlight ever again. Children of overbearing parents may develop anxiety (I'm not actually as great as Mom thinks, someone will find out I'm faking), depression (I'm so tired and I can't try anymore), substance abuse problems (I don't even know who I am, maybe something can help me), and eating disorders (to be anything less than perfect will destroy me).

If the parent isn't outright controlling and pulling the social strings, they may be overparenting as a helicopter parent. Just as Millennials have their share of HuffPo and Buzzfeed articles, so do the children of overbearing helicopter parents. Of course, many times these groups are one and the same.

> *"The parents of most Millennials are either Baby Boomers or, for the younger Millennials, Gen Xers. This need for verbal approval and reinforcement correlates with the way detached parenting was normalized in the 1960s*

and '70s, when Boomers grew up. As a result of not being babied or supervised themselves as children, as well as cultural shifts in parenting norms through the progression of technology, these generations overcompensated in their involvement with their Millennial children. Thus, "helicopter parents" were created."[14]

–Ilana Bodker, How Baby Boomer Parents Molded the Millennial Generation

Adult children of helicopter parents often call their parents for advice before decisions. Not just big decisions about buying a home or getting married, but any decision or question, like how long something is supposed to go into the microwave or thinking about changing a hairstyle. They're also often perfectionists who have an almost pathological need to achieve more and more, but these achievements are more likely to make their parents feel proud or satisfied than the actual person doing the work.

Unfortunately, and very confusingly, helicopter parents of adult children will try to become friends or buddies with their grown kids rather than maintaining a healthy psychological (or even physical) distance. While it can be comforting knowing that Mom and Dad are just a phone call away, it's not always healthy. In ages past, when a young adult graduated high school and started college, their parents would drop them at the dorms with their books and their duffel bag before scooting on home and sending a letter or two before seeing them for a semester break. These days, we have email and Facebook and cell phones and parents can keep tabs on their kids, even though they're no longer "kids," from afar, in an instant.

In a 2013 study at California State University, Fresno, management professors Jill C. Bradley-Geist and Julie B. Olson-Buchanan explored the consequences of helicopter parenting.[15] In their review of existing research, they found studies indicating a positive correlation between helicopter parenting and anxiety, depression, and low self-esteem...*in two- and four-year-old children* (emphasis mine). Also discovered was a correlation between helicopter parenting and neuroticism and dependency. Helicopter parenting is also associated with recreational use of pain medications and taking prescription medication for anxiety and depression.

To really drive home that the challenges of the helicopter-parented children and the challenges of the Millennial are intricately linked, there is also research linking over-parenting and entitlement mentality.[16] What else can you expect for a generation raised without the opportunity to struggle and learn from their mistakes? When you've gone from age zero to eighteen with your parents doing everything for you, is it any wonder that the world now accuses you of being an entitled narcissist?

Back to the Bradley-Geist and Olson-Buchanan research at California State. Their survey of college students explored general parental involvement and over-parenting as they correlate to various work-related outcomes. Students with overly-involved parents were found to have lower social and general self-efficacy, as well as "maladaptive responses to workplace scenarios." Those who had been raised with a helicopter parenting style were more likely to choose workplace solutions that relied on someone else, rather than taking personal responsibility.

"Without a strong sense of self-efficacy, or the belief that
one can accomplish tasks and goals, young adults are likely
to be dependent on others, engage in poor coping strategies,
and fail to take accountability in the workplace." So, what's a
grown adult to do, when they realize they've been raised to be
essentially helpless?

If you were raised by helicopter parents (or, more likely, a
helicopter *parent,* as single parenthood correlates with over-
parenting), all is not lost. You are not merely an entitled blob
of dependent workplace goo, waiting for a group project you
can hide behind. There is hope for you to become a functional
adult in society and avoid harming the development of your own
children. This is the ultimate danger of toxic parenting: in an
attempt to avoid hurting your children the way you were hurt,
you run the risk of swinging the pendulum too far in the opposite
direction, hurting them anyway. It happens with parenting just
like it happens on a societal scale, one generation blaming the
next because they don't understand why their efforts didn't do
what they wanted.

Adverse Childhood Experiences

One of the most well-known studies related to childhood
trauma is the Adverse Childhood Experiences (ACE) study
first conducted by the CDC and Kaiser-Permanente from 1995
to 1997.[17] The ACE study investigated the correlation between
adverse experiences in a subject's childhood and negative
outcomes later in life. The more ACEs someone experienced as a
child, the more risk they have for outcomes such as alcohol abuse,

depression, illicit drug use, and suicide attempts. There is also a correlation linking ACEs to early initiation of sexual activity, higher risk for domestic violence, higher risk of sexual violence, and increased rates of sexually transmitted infections, adolescent and unintended pregnancies, and fetal death. Similarly, there is an increased risk for smoking (including early initiation of smoking), and health outcomes like liver disease, heart disease, and pulmonary disease. Finally, factors such as poor work performance, financial stress, and poor academic achievement are also linked with ACEs.

What are the ACEs?

The ACEs studied in the late 1990s are common and affect children into their adulthood, possibly for their entire lives. These experiences include:

- Physical abuse
- Sexual abuse
- Emotional abuse
- Physical neglect
- Emotional neglect
- Mother treated violently
- Household substance abuse
- Household mental illness
- Parental separation or divorce
- Incarcerated household member

I believe that traumatic childhood circumstances are linked to the perception that Millennials are entitled and narcissistic. The Baby Boomer Generation skyrocketed the divorce rate in the

United States, and divorced parents are one of the ACEs studied. Obviously not every child of divorced parents was neglected or abused, but a divorce is almost always emotionally traumatic. Add to the general trauma of a divorce other ACEs, like witnessing domestic violence or alcohol abuse in the household, and the effect snowballs quickly from a couple of ACEs to a whole pile of them. It can be argued that the Boomer Generation was one of the first that made it socially acceptable to divorce, and I'd argue that they were victim to plenty of ACEs themselves. As we continue to name and study these factors, it's easier to see the pattern has repeated itself for generations.

Imagine that someone born in the 1950s grew up with either ignoring or engulfing parents. They may have grown up with corporal punishment or been forced to "respect their elders" even if their elders were toxic toward them. Or they may have been a golden child, loved and adored and allowed to do whatever they pleased, but suffering from the lack of boundaries. They may have had to tiptoe around alcoholism, or maybe they tried to ignore domestic violence in the home.

These children grew up and got married and had kids of their own, and maybe they struggled to find a balance between preserving the idyllic parts of their own childhoods and trying to ensure their children had a better life in other ways. As the prevalence of divorce expanded, and as women developed more agency and financial independence, the times were definitely a-changing.

The Baby Boomers didn't know what to do. Nothing was the same as it used to be. They were growing up during the sexual revolution and had better access to birth control. Feminism was gaining more and more traction, as Baby Boomer women made up 45 percent of the labor force and overtook men in the completion of college degrees. In the midst of all this change, how were the Boomers to effectively raise the next generation?

Part of working through your own childhood traumas with the help of a trained therapist is to put yourself in the shoes of your parents and understand the source of their behavior. This does not mean you have to forgive them, but it can be helpful in understanding that it's not your fault. Your parents were not perfectly healthy and well-adapted people who mistreated you because of something inherently wrong with you. They were mistreated as well, as were their parents before them. It does not excuse what happened to you, but it gives greater context.

Abuse is never the victim's fault. When we begin to understand that this applies on a generational scale as well as an individual one, we can see how to break the cycle of generational blame. It's not that Millennials are suddenly a group of whining, spoiled, entitled brats. Generation X was called a generation of lazy slackers. Boomers had their own challenges from the generation before them. Each generation is prone to lose their own context and ability to relate to the younger crowd when society starts heaping all the blame on the next generation. Let's stop the cycle.

Solutions for Adult Children of Emotionally Abusive Parents

First, understand that it's not your fault if your parents ignored or overprotected you. It was nothing wrong or broken within you that caused their behavior. It is okay to acknowledge that your parents hurt you. In fact, they actively impeded your development, independence, and autonomy. You deserve to figure out your own way in life, and you will not feel fulfilled by following someone else's prescribed path for you or spending your life chasing someone's approval.

Begin to distance yourself from your parents and set boundaries with them. Depending on their level of involvement in your life, this might be as easy as not always picking up the phone when they call, or it might be as hard as having to sit them down and explain that you need some space. I also implore you to find a good therapist who can help you sift through your brain and establish boundaries with your parents.

It's possible that, with a lot of work on boundaries and open lines of communication, you can reconcile with your parents. However, a fundamental part of reconciliation is their willingness to admit they harmed you. If they insist that they did nothing wrong or make excuses about why they behaved the way they did, you may end up spending years of your life in the same cycles with them.

Good parents practice unconditional love. They don't threaten to disown their children or change their locks if somebody comes home with a nose ring. (True story.)

How to Make Sure You're Killing It

Talk to your child self. One thing you can do, if you have leftover childhood tapes playing loops in your brain and getting in your way, is to dig up an old photo of yourself as a kid. Tape it to your mirror, keep it in your wallet, or snap a photo of it on your smartphone. Now comes the fun part: Talk to yourself as a child. Go back to those moments when your parents or other trusted adults said or did something to you that created a wound in your life. Pretend that you have come upon a child crying over those very things, and comfort the child. Tell the child that it is not their fault, and that they are not worthless, they are not doomed to be alone for their entire life, they are not only worth something if a man loves them. Give the child your love, and understand that it wasn't your fault.

Act like Spock. This was one thing I did when I started to distance myself from my mother. I just acted like I was an alien or researcher on an investigative mission, observing my mother's behavior through the lens of someone who didn't have a history with her. I was able to keep my distance and avoid getting worked up emotionally over things she said to me, because I had this researcher hat on instead of letting her get to me with her not-so-subtle criticisms.

Decide on your boundaries. What you will accept from other people is up to you. If they can't listen, kick them out of your life. Spend some time deciding what you will and will not accept from people, especially your parents. If they're still calling you a childhood nickname you don't want to go by, tell them. If they insist on calling you the name even though you've asked them not to, they're violating a boundary. It's a small boundary, but it's a boundary just the same. Communicate your boundaries and stick to them.

Do your homework. Reading books about toxic parents and childhood abuse can be extremely helpful in understanding the ways your childhood experiences shaped your behavior as an adult. I've been reading books like this for over five years and still uncover something new with each new title I read. Some of my favorites include *Will I Ever Be Good Enough? Healing the Daughters of Narcissistic Mothers* by Karyl McBride, *Toxic Parents* by Susan Forward, and *Daughter Detox* by Peg Streep.

There is no such thing as perfect. You might cut contact with a parent or family member and then end up running into them, having to see them at a family event, or otherwise initiating contact again. This doesn't mean you've screwed up or you have to start all over again. Go back to the level of contact that feels good for you and don't worry that you didn't do it perfectly. You're fine. You're doing awesome.

Chapter 3

Millennials Are Killing the Workplace

"Did Millennials Kill the 9-to-5 Workday, or Just Point Out That It's Dead?"

–*Entrepreneur*, **March 2016**

"Working with Millennials is the worst"

–*New York Post*, **September 2016**

When I applied for my current job, the woman who would become my new boss wrote me an email inviting me for a phone interview. She happened to mention that the company offered flexible scheduling and work-from-home days, which she correctly assumed would be a big draw for me, since the job included a hefty commute. I spoke with her on the phone, and we already got along great before I came in for my in-person interview. I left the building feeling confident and super-excited.

Then I hit a deer and totaled my car on the way home. I decided to take this as a sign to keep moving forward, rather than a sign that this was a terrible job for me. Like the Universe was saying, "You sure about a new job, buddy? That's a real long commute." Alas, the pull of the quirky college town, along with the fact that I negotiated a pretty bitchin' salary raise over my previous role, were enough to sway me with very little arm-twisting.

When I started the new gig, I asked with some anxiety and hesitation if it would be okay if I went home at four instead of five, so I could leave while it was still daylight. Winter's short days are a giant downer anyway, even if you haven't recently crashed the car you've had for eight years right into a buck. My manager, still super-excited to have me on board and assure me that the deer was not a sign of my impending doom with the company, readily agreed.

Even though some employers grumble about the entitled Millennials wanting flextime and work-from-home opportunities, it turns out that flexible schedules aren't that hard to offer employees! And the employees really appreciate it! Who would have thought, right?

There's been an explosion in flexible schedules in what used to be standard nine-to-five workplaces, including perks like telecommuting and flextime. It's not just Millennials taking advantage of these growing trends, but of course the responsibility rests with us if you listen to the media headlines, like the one from *Entrepreneur* referenced at the head of this chapter.

A 2014 survey at Bentley University reports that Millennials "believe that flexible work schedules make the workplace more productive for people their age," and workplace research tends to back this up.[18] *Forbes* and *Inc.* report articles linking flexible schedules to improved employee morale and productivity. In fact, work-life balance and company culture makes a bigger impact to Millennials than salary itself.

Check out some of these stats:

- "Millennials would take an average pay cut of $7,600 if they could improve their career development, find more purposeful work, better work-life balance, or a better company culture."[19]

- "Millennials as well as men were most likely…to say that they would take a pay cut, forgo a promotion or be willing to move to manage work-life demands better."[20]

- "Lack of flexibility was cited among the top reasons Millennials quit jobs."[21]

- "Forty-three percent of Millennials envision leaving their jobs within two years; only 28 percent seek to stay beyond five years… Attracting and retaining Millennials and Gen Z respondents begins with financial rewards and workplace culture; it is enhanced when the workplace offers higher degrees of flexibility."[22]

The fact is, people are willing to put in time and energy for a company that lets them balance work and life more effectively.

Most of the trouble comes in because the younger generations, including Millennials and the upcoming Generation Z, as well as many from Generation X, don't know how to negotiate for what they're worth (or even that negotiation of a job is on the table at all). The advice from the older crowd is to get your foot in the door and be indispensable, but nobody is indispensable, so why not chase a career that lights your fire *and* pays the bills?

When it comes to the progression of a career, there is a vast generation gap. Older generations tended to start a career out of college and stay in one profession (or even one company) for the duration of their professional life, enjoying a steady progression of routine reviews and scheduled pay raises. Meanwhile, the next generation of professionals tends to job-hop and build a diverse portfolio and resume in their search for rewarding and fulfilling work.

To put these work trends into pop-culture perspective, consider the Gilmore family, from the television show *Gilmore Girls*. (Am I dating myself? I don't care. I'll be Grandma Millennial today.) Lorelai Gilmore is estranged from her wealthy parents at the start of the series, having run away from them and their high-class lifestyle when she became a teen mother to her daughter Rory. She left home and found work as a maid in a small-town inn, working her way up to management and later opening her own inn. Lorelai's mother Emily did not work outside the home, and her father Richard worked for an insurance company for his entire career. When discussing the direction Lorelai's life took,

Richard Gilmore says that she could have married Christopher (Rory's father) and Richard would have put him to work at the insurance company. Lorelai protests that Christopher didn't want that life and neither did she.

This is the disconnect between older generations and younger generations. Baby Boomers were largely content to get a stable, secure job and put in their decades of service until retirement. Millennials want and need more from their work. Millennials prefer to work in organizations with a meaningful (i.e., not bullshit) mission statement that do something to better the global community.

Back in the *Gilmore Girls* world, Rory Gilmore attends a private prep school with the hopes of attending Harvard and becoming a journalist. Unfortunately, in the 2016 Netflix revival of the series, Rory doesn't display the hardworking sentiments of the self-made Millennial. She's become a journalist, and a celebrated one at that. But she's also an entitled and privileged white woman who expects to ride her acclaim and reputation into a job interview without preparing at all, and she's shocked to not receive a job offer on the sole basis of being Rory Gilmore. We watched in abject horror as the lovable, likeable, wonderful Rory of our young teen years grew up and shined a retroactive spotlight on the privilege we didn't notice when we watched the show in middle school.

To create the career you want, you do in fact need to put some work into it. But how do you balance the cycle of needing a job to get experience, while needing experience to get hired for a job?

The Rise of the Unpaid Internship

Herein lies the problem of modern job-seekers: Whether college-educated or not, younger workers are often offered experience or exposure in lieu of wages. The unpaid internship is a popular way to bring fresh workers into a company without affecting the bottom line, and young professionals who struggle to advance in their fields become more and more willing to take unpaid work as they plan a career trajectory.

But giving away your time and energy in exchange for experience doesn't necessarily help you when it comes time to pay the bills—especially if you end up doing something completely unrelated to what you thought you'd be doing.

Even now that I make a good salary working in marketing and have a growing freelance writing business, I still get pitches to work for the low, low price of experience. Huffington Post reached out to me the day I published the original Gaslighting blog post and wanted to re-publish it on their website. When I asked about compensation, I was told that they don't pay their contributors, but that their robust audience would result in more new views and visitors to my site. I also received an email from a literary agent, which is why you're reading this real, actual book instead of retweeting my blog post from HuffPo.

Some people have the income and security to be able to scoff at an unpaid opportunity for exposure, but others without a full-time career or who are trying to get a foothold in a new industry will likely feel trapped into giving away their time and effort for free. And that's another nail in the coffin of people taking Millennials seriously. If you're willing to work for nothing, you must not be worth a living wage. But when you demand a living wage or dare to complain, you're told to take what you can get and be grateful. The goal posts are constantly moving, and there is no way to stay ahead of the game when the rules keep changing.

This disconnect is especially stark in the world of the work-from-home entrepreneur. I am friends with people who craft and sell their wares online, for prices that seem exorbitant compared to what you can buy off the rack at your local discount store. But they're not selling stuff off the rack, they're hand-creating something just for you, and they've put years of their life into their craft. If you want a hat for fifteen bucks, go buy one for fifteen bucks. If you want a custom-knit, prop-realistic fourth Doctor scarf, expect to pony up some cash.

Make no mistake: Your skills and time have value and worth. You deserve compensation for your work, whatever it is.

Millennial Entrepreneurs

Many young professionals give up on the tedium of trying to find the corporate fit that's right for them and end up creating their own careers and companies. Whether it's a side gig or a full-time labor of love, creating your own business is a legitimate way to build your professional career and your income. If you have a skill, there's someone out there willing to pay for it.

Your skill might be writing, installing security systems, cleaning houses, or walking dogs. You might be great at graphic design or a self-taught cook who can create customized allergy-friendly meal plans. Maybe you've found fitness as a young adult and you can help others create a gym routine or home fitness routine that works for them. Or you might be an excellent craftsman who builds and installs custom cabinets and shelving units.

My advice to budding entrepreneurs is the same as my advice to those considering a college education: work smarter and don't go into debt. Start with small and manageable projects that you can do in your free time while you build a market for yourself through word of mouth and local advertising. However, if you can't find the job you want in the workforce, it's absolutely an option to create your own and start a business.

While there is no lack of Diem to Carpe in this entrepreneurial world, I see time and time again how people starting out in business for themselves end up devaluing their own work. They'll price their wares low to make a sale, but it's often not enough to cover materials and create a profit on their time and energy. It's not just the workforce that devalues young workers; we're even doing it to ourselves.

I once massively underestimated the time it would take me to complete a set of commissioned paintings and essentially gave them away. I could have charged three times as much and felt good about the sale, but I had figured they'd be quick and simple. I was wrong.

It was also a huge emotional gamble for me to raise my freelance rates to something more in line with my experience level. I had started at fifteen dollars per hour, then twenty, and finally twenty-five. After working at this rate for over a year, and adding a full year's worth of full-time marketing and writing experience to my resume, I decided it was time for a price adjustment. But I took a deep breath and went big—I raised my rates to forty dollars an hour. My clients didn't skip a beat and readily agreed to the new rates, leaving me to wonder how long I had been selling myself short and keeping myself in the bargain bin. For what it's worth, forty dollars is still a bargain in the freelance copywriting world. I've seen some estimates that say a freelance writer shouldn't charge less than fifty to one hundred dollars per hour, depending on their experience.

Long story short, get out there with your amazing skills and make some money, if that's what you want to do. If you prefer to stay in the mainstream workplace, something new and unique will probably pop up soon to offer a new way to showcase your expertise.

Get some inspiration from these Millennial entrepreneurs:

Robyn Rihanna Fenty: Yes—*the* Rihanna! She launched the cosmetic line Fenty Beauty at age twenty-nine—without a college degree. Fenty caters to every skin tone, giving women of color actual options in the mainstream makeup game.

Katie Sones: As a college junior, Katie got the idea for her makeup business Lipslut on the day of Donald Trump's inauguration. Fifty percent of profits benefit progressive and human rights charities. Its inaugural color was "F*ck Trump."

Apoorva Mehta: With a degree in electrical engineering, Apoorva started approximately twenty different companies before he founded Instacart, which provides same-day delivery of groceries (and lets people pick up a side gig with good tips!).

Cashmere Nicole: After four and a half years and a breast cancer diagnosis, Cashmere almost gave up on her passion project, makeup brand Beauty Bakerie. But then she started seeing traction and the brand exploded almost overnight (you know, a night that lasted about five years). She quit her day job as a nurse to focus on the company full-time.

Whitney Wolfe Herd: If you know how to swipe right, you know Whitney's creations. She's the co-founder of Tinder and the founder and CEO of Bumble. Her degree is in International Studies.

Guadalupe Jones: A former US Marine and Mexico native, Guadalupe launched Fluffaholic at age twenty-nine. Fluffaholic is an online retailer of sustainable and natural baby and maternity clothing, toys, and gear.

Rosie Wiklund: Creating a custom clothing company out of your home is no small feat, but sewist Rosie has grown their brand and can barely keep clothes in stock. From bikinis to embroidered sweaters to the comfiest dresses and even "naw bras" (a supportive but not torturous boob-wrangler), Rosie's brand Cute Thing and Pun is one of a kind. And so is everything you'll buy from them.

Amanda Thomas: A chance encounter with a buyer from Fred Segal turned Amanda's after-school side gig into a full-fledged accessory line at the age of only sixteen. Amanda later graduated from Otis College of Art and Design, and she continues to develop her national brand, Luv Aj.

Elise Hennigan: Combining a love of dogs with a creative idea and business savvy, Elise is the creator behind Should We Go? training tools and gear for dogs, including a hands-free dog leash that attaches at the waist (your waist, not the dog's).

If you have an idea, and you're willing to put in some time, you can make your own entrepreneurial endeavors a success. But if you don't want to, that's just as valid.

A Changing Workforce

Millennials (and the generations after us) face a rapidly changing workforce as new companies are born into the economy daily. Startups can get their initial capital from crowdfunding websites like IndieGoGo and Kickstarter, and Millennials are happy to pitch in to get a great new idea off the ground. Some ideas even make it to popular business television shows like *Shark Tank*, such as organic fruit snack company Peaceful Fruits, based in Akron, Ohio. Peaceful Fruits founder Evan Delahanty said in his *Shark Tank* episode, "Social enterprise is the future of business." Though the company didn't get picked for a deal on the popular TV show, sales on the air date were more than 200 percent of all of 2016's sales. You don't even have to get your idea picked for investment, as long as people see it. Those who believe in your mission will follow you.

As Millennials adapt to the new economy and social currency, they are finding amazing ways to make a living while helping and educating others. That "lazy, entitled" Millennial next door might be:

- Starting a business to improve their local community.

- Selling online courses based on the skills they have developed in the workforce and from college or training classes.

- Self-publishing books, blogs, vlogs, and podcasts to educate the masses.

Whether you're taking the entrepreneurial route or sticking with the nine-to-five (albeit a flexible nine-to-five), advancing in your career is all about how you present yourself.

Resumes, Cover Letters, and Interviews

Are you one of those people who could never do sales? You can't stand the idea of feeling like a slimy used-car dude in a tiny lot, pressuring someone to buy now, right now, before this deal is no longer available. You know the guy is just itching for a commission, and you feel super creeped-out.

I have good news and bad news. The bad news is that landing a job interview, getting hired, and negotiating within your company are all about being in sales. The product you're selling is yourself and your experience. The good news is: You can totally do this without feeling like a slimy creep. It's all in the presentation.

If you don't need resume help, feel free to skip this section. If you do need resume help, you're welcome!

The Resume

If you have varied work experience (including paid and unpaid work), it can be intimidating to try to create a resume without looking like you've hopped around between fields and jobs at random. The easiest way to make this look good is to consult a professional resume writer who can help you organize your experience in a way that highlights your relevant skill set. You can expect to spend anywhere from $50–$150 on a professional resume.

If that's not in your budget, that's okay too. You can DIY this thing with just a couple of hours of your time and a few basic guidelines. You'll be designing a functional resume that combines your most relevant experience with a list of your skills and credentials, rather than a traditional chronological list of jobs and duties throughout the years. By organizing your resume this way (which I recommend everyone do, not just those with a job-hop employment history), you highlight the most important aspects of your expertise that align with the job you're applying for.

When working on your resume, keep the following in mind. Some of this advice will go against a typical resume template. I make my own rules, and people get jobs with my resumes. You do you, though. I'm not the boss of you.

You have less than ten seconds. Assume that you have less than ten seconds with a recruiter or hiring manager's eyes on your resume. Put the most relevant and intriguing content at the top of the resume to hook them and get them to read the rest in more detail.

Tailor your resume. You should have a unique resume for nearly every application. Tweaking a few things can present your work history in a completely new light that's tailored to each individual employer. Review the job description and make a list of the things the employer wants that you've done in the past, even if it wasn't in a similar role. You're presenting your skills and experience, which is much more important than the job title you had when you learned or applied the skill. Make sure your resume includes every one of those common factors from the job posting.

Skip the objective. I love to replace the traditional objective (which always boils down to "to get a job that pays me money so I can eat") with a professional profile instead. This profile is one to two sentences, like: *Marketing professional with a passion for creating content that tells a story and engages a community to take meaningful action; seeking a position with a small local business to help grow brand mission and create a positive impact.* This profile gets right to the point: the applicant has a marketing background and likes to focus on small businesses that are mission-driven and support a community. This shows the reader two things, that the applicant has what they need and that they have what the applicant wants.

Include a skills section. Make a list of industry-appropriate skills in alphabetical order for easy scanning. Go through the job description and pull out any skills listed that you can match on your resume.

List relevant and unique experience. My first job was operating a cash register and making soft-serve cones at Dairy Queen when I was seventeen. This is no longer on my resume. You don't have to list every job you've ever had, but you should list anything relevant. Include your job title, company name, dates worked there (month and year), and location of the company. If you want (or if you need to fill a little space), add a one-sentence description of the company below these key details. When you're listing out your job duties, avoid saying "responsible for" and don't use the same bullet points for each job. I don't care if you operated a cash register and provided customer service at three different jobs, find a new way to say it.

Avoid "Responsible for." This one may have gotten lost in the shuffle of the last point, so I'm saying it again. If you were responsible for cashing out at the end of the night, or you were responsible for maintaining a database of magazine articles, or you were responsible for serving snacks at a daycare, how is the employer going to know you actually did it? What if you were responsible for it but just didn't care one day, and no toddlers got their graham crackers? Tell the employer what you did. Actions! The above examples easily become "oversaw cashing out of all registers upon closing," "developed and maintained an up-to-date database of magazine queries and publications," and "served age-appropriate meals and snacks according to nutrition guidelines." Damn, don't you sound fancy.

Don't use Times New Roman. Play around with some fonts but avoid anything too far out of the realm of average. No curly letters or handwriting fonts, unless it's a serious design commitment that matches the brand you're applying for. Speaking of which, if you can use any fonts similar to the company logo, try spicing things up with that in the header with your name. Don't go nuts. My recommended font choices are Georgia, Cambria, and Book Antiqua. Arial and Verdana are alright too, I just personally prefer serifs for my professional documents.

You don't need your whole address. Putting your address on a resume hearkens back to the olden days when people didn't have email. Employers would mail things to your house. Weird, right? Nowadays you can just include your city and state, along with your phone number and email address.

Make sure you have a professional email address. Your first and last name is a safe bet. Just be smart about it.

The Cover Letter

In addition to your resume, a solid cover letter is an absolute must, and it should include three basic sections, which I will now describe in significantly less excruciating detail than the resume advice above.

Introduction and how you found the job posting. "Dear Ms. So-and-So, I found the job posting for XYZ position on Indeed.com and I've attached my resume to formally apply for the position."

Outline of your relevant skills and why you're the right man for the job. "Working at ABC company, I have learned to perform high-quality work on tight deadlines, and I manage a team of three employees."

Conclusion, appreciation, and contact information. "I look forward to discussing my qualifications with you in the coming weeks and appreciate the opportunity to apply for a position with your company. I can be reached at 555-5555 or YourEmailHere@gmail.com to schedule an interview."

The Interview

Look at you go, badass! You got an interview with that rockin' resume and cover letter. Now what? I've applied to a lot more jobs than I've interviewed for, and I've interviewed for a lot more jobs than I've gotten. However, the three positions I have successfully gotten since I started working full-time at age twenty-three felt like done deals once I got the interview.

Bring copies of your resume. No one will need them, but have them anyway. You don't have to get the fancy paper.

Make a PowerPoint. You don't have to use it in your interview, but if you take some time to create a pitch or presentation about yourself and how you're the right person for the role, it helps. I don't know how or why it helps, but I've always felt more prepared when I've taken the time to highlight my skills in a professional way, long before I make it to the interview. I suspect that the act of looking at my resume objectively to bring out the best parts for my pitch helps me realize I'm selling a skill set and must get my confident sales face on. (PS: I usually present the PowerPoint in my interviews and it has always delighted my managers, who assume I am always this organized.)

Prepare, but don't panic. Prepare for the interview questions everybody knows. "Tell me a little about yourself" means you tell them about your career and what your job passions are (NOT your life story). "What's your greatest strength? What about your greatest weakness?" means, tell them something you're proud of doing and something you can hide inside a positive, like hiding a pill in a piece of cheese for your dog. "My greatest strength is my organizational and PowerPoint-making abilities. My greatest weakness is that I sometimes take on more than I can handle because I always want to say yes." They know that's kind of a bullshit answer you found on the internet, so don't be surprised if they skip this question entirely. I want you to prepare for the questions that make you want to stare at the interviewer, silently mouthing "What?" When you get asked questions like this, don't panic. "I can see that you're able to stay calm under stress. What makes you angry at work?" "What is your favorite type of restaurant?" "What is your opinion of the Oxford comma?" Good responses to such questions should be honest. "I got upset with a boss when my idea was rejected and then brought back later, when someone else said it." "I love all foods, especially Mexican." "Oxford comma for LIFE."

Say thank you. I will not let Millennials kill the thank-you note. Send off an email after your interview thanking the interviewer for their time spent chatting with you about the role. Say something truly profesh like, "After talking with you, I feel even more strongly that I'm a great match for your company." And then give two or three bullet points about why you're such a good match.

The Offer

You got the job, congrats! My first two job offers, I just took. I was so thrilled to get the offer, I took the offer without any counter. With both jobs, I was desperate for the role and basically would have taken anything. The third job, I didn't need to switch. I was happy where I was. So, when they offered me the job and it was literally my pie-in-the-sky dream offer that I didn't think I'd get, I asked a friend what to do. Her advice was amazing, and I shall include it along with advice of my own.

A man would do it. Would the average man negotiate and counter his offer? You bet your ass he would. Men have the inherent confidence of knowing they have power, and so often we don't feel very confident or powerful when a company is extending an offer. From our perspective, this company has chosen to take a giant risk on you, and they're willing to pay you this much money, and you're just so grateful to have been chosen, you don't even read the benefits package. From the company's perspective, though, the hiring process sucks, and by the time they make an offer, they want you. They really, really want you. They probably want you a couple more thousand dollars than that. Counter. Here's an easy way to do it: "Wow, this is such a generous offer, I appreciate it so much. I'd be thrilled to come aboard, but I still need a few days to make my final decision. However, it would be an easy yes for me if the salary was more in this range." Send it off and wait. If they can't swing it, they'll tell you the original offer stands. I've never heard of a company rescinding an offer in response to a counter. If they can afford the bump and still get what they want (you!), they'll meet you there, or at least halfway.

Respond promptly. You can ask for a few days to officially accept, or they may have a timeline on the offer. Take all the time you need, but try not to push it to the last minute. If you've decided on a Wednesday but you're worried about telling your current boss so soon, take a deep breath, send off the acceptance letter, and go tell your boss.

Telling your boss is awful. The first time I ever gave notice was at the Dairy Queen job I had when I was seventeen. I said, "Hey John, guess what?" and one of the managers turned to look at me and said, "What?" I threw my hands in the air excitedly and squealed, "I'm quitting!" Then I asked him if he wanted me to finish out my week's schedule, and he said, yes, that would be really nice of me. Apparently, most people don't actually give notice at their fast-food job. The second time I gave notice was crushing, because my temp agency insisted on telling my manager and said I couldn't do it. So, I had to watch my manager, who adored me, walk past me into her office and take the phone call that I was leaving. Next up, I gave notice in a way that was stressful, because my off-site director tended to tell people to take a hike right then and there, but my on-site manager wanted me to finish out the month to help with inventory. I ended up staying through inventory, but the manager had to personally tell the director he needed me. And the last time I gave notice, to start the job with the deer and the totaled car, I cried and sobbed my way through giving my notice. I loved, loved, loved that boss. She was an incredible manager and is still a wonderful friend. I felt like I was letting her down, but I also knew that I just got an amazing offer and I had to take it. She was, of course, understanding and super happy for me, because she is amazing and not at all petty. Love you, Jaime!

Write a resignation letter. Keep it short, to the point, and professional. "Dear boss, I have accepted an offer from another company and must resign. I am giving two weeks' notice and my last day will be…"—you get the idea. Of course, if you are close with your supervisor and have a friendly relationship, you can include such lines as "This is breaking my heart," and "I am devastated but rolling in the dough now."

Don't gloat. Yes, you only have ten, nine, eight, seven days left to work in this place, but don't do a little dance about it. You like your coworkers, remember? Except whoever let the milk go bad in the fridge. Gloat about that instead, and pray you don't have a salmon microwaver at the next place.

How to Make Sure You're Killing It

Your career path is up to you and the direction you want to follow. If you want to work in an office, great. If you want to start a business, great. You don't even have to know right now—but you do have to know that your work is valuable. Time is money, and you're worth getting paid for your time.

First impressions matter. Keep your resume and professional profiles like LinkedIn up to date and consider making different versions for different types of positions. Dress up for your interview.

Don't be scared to ask about benefits. When interviewing for a job, it's okay to ask about flexible scheduling options and other perks. The worst they can say is no.

Know your worth. Comparison-shop yourself and your expertise with peers in your field, whether that's how much to charge for a crocheted pony or salary requirements for someone with three years' experience in your field.

Plan for expenses. Remember self-employment taxes are a doozy, and save your receipts and roughly 25 percent of your self-employment income.

Get some help. Hiring a skills coach can help you launch a startup or advance in your current career.

Chapter 4

Millennials Are Killing Education

"If There's One Thing Millennials Regret, It's Going to College"

—*Forbes*, **August 2016**

"Why Are So Many Millennials Dropping Out of College?"

—**Jeff Selingo, April 2016**

"Generation Dropout: Millennials Joining the Workforce Are Less Educated Than Retiring Boomers"

—*The Atlantic*, **June 2013**

I picked the perfect college for me: small, liberal arts based, in a small town, close enough to home to visit on the weekends but not so close my parents would show up without warning. I was freshly dating my first love and was excited for all the new experiences, friendships, and education that college would bring. It was a great time in my life. And I, like so many others, am still paying off the loans.

Millennials on the whole have proved to be a booming success for higher education. Statistics from the Pew Research Center indicate that we're the most educated generation, meaning more of us graduated from college than other generations. Pew posits that "Some of the 'credit' for recent increases [in college graduation] appears to go to the Great Recession of 2007–2009 and the sluggish jobs recovery since. With young adults facing sharply diminished labor market opportunities, their rate of high school and college completion has been rising slowly but steadily since 2007, after having been stagnant during better economic times earlier in the decade."[23]

We're making more money with our bachelor's degrees than past generations, and even more with postgraduate degrees like master's degrees and doctorates. However, the center continues, "Admittedly, the earnings figures above only reflect young adults who can find work."[24] Further research into household income and socioeconomic factors doesn't indicate that the boost in income was causally linked to college education, but rather suggests that having a college education leads to other "economic payoffs" in the long run.

More Millennials have attended college than in previous generations and are even more educated than our Gen X and Boomer counterparts on the whole, but we still risk high dropout rates—and the associated student loans, regardless of graduation status. A recent update from Student Loan Hero says that "Americans are more burdened by student loan debt than ever" and points to some $1.4 trillion in student loan debt across the nation.[25]

When we're told over and over again that we need an education to get a job, our options are limited. We either don't go to college, work to pay cash for college, or take out massive student loan debt to pay for college. The normalization of student loans as "good debt" is one more way younger generations have been sold a bill of goods they can't really afford. With skyrocketing tuition costs, how are we supposed to keep up?

Let's kill higher education! (Not really. But maybe a little bit.)

In my life, it was never a question of *if* I would go to college one day, it was a definite plan. Test scores, extracurricular activities, high school jobs, and AP level classes were just part of the deal. Only now, looking back on my own privileged life, can I see that others didn't have it so planned out. Some young adults dream about attending college but never make it, while others couldn't care less about going.

I came home from college fairs with enormous stacks of brochures and made pro-con lists on poster boards, creating a matrix of characteristics I wanted in my ideal college. I'm sure tuition cost was on that list somewhere, but I barely registered it. You just get loans for that, silly, who cares! (Spoiler alert: I should have cared.) Thanks to the Pell Grant, various minor scholarships, and one very hefty scholarship, I graduated with my bachelor's degree in three years with about twenty thousand dollars in student loan debt. I could have stopped there. Instead I skipped right along to graduate school, where I studied Higher Education Administration and Student Personnel, with the hopes of working in college housing and residence life.

Though tuition at the public Kent State University is much cheaper than tuition at my private undergrad, Wilmington College, I ended up with forty thousand more dollars in student loan debt because I decided "working on my education" was more important than actually working. I quit my part-time job as a day care assistant and focused on school, maxing out my loans and living off the excess. Did I mention I was a newlywed and had just financed a car? My husband had three part-time jobs, and my sole income was a $600 per month stipend from a part-time graduate assistantship. The car payment was $324. I was racking up a $1,000 balance each month on a credit card to "build my credit" and paid it off out of my checking account, which was full of borrowed money for school. Paying off unnecessary debt with borrowed money is kind of my financial low point.

After graduation, I looked for jobs in my field, but, despite having experience with first-year programs, residence life, academic advising, and career counseling, I didn't receive any job offers after submitting over a hundred applications and having roughly twenty interviews. I ended up living with my mom while going through a divorce and temping as a receptionist in a real estate office before getting my first full-time job as a specialty chemical purchaser, which was nowhere on my radar of possible professions.

During this time, I had also become a freelance writer working on blogs and social media. I later decided I wanted to be a full-time writer, so I made another career change after three years in purchasing. Now I write full time, in addition to my freelance writing on the side.

Do you want to know the best part of my entire journey? Halfway through graduate school, when I finally started to think about having children and a family, I realized I'd like to be a stay-at-home mom. It's hard to do that when you have sixty thousand dollars in student loan debt with an interest rate twice the going rate of a mortgage.

The truth of the matter, and the point of this long winding story, is this: My degree wasn't necessary to prepare me for my career.

We expect students to enroll in college and pick a major and career path the instant they reach adulthood. If they decide to take time between high school and college, or decide not to attend at all, society heaps stigma upon them for not being educated, despite the fact that they may be making an excellent salary at a skilled trade or as a successful entrepreneur with no need for a college degree.

A college education is not a necessity. It certainly isn't a guarantee of income or success.

If you *want* to attend college, that is a noble and valid choice. Do it wisely. If you *don't want* to attend college, that is a noble and valid choice. Do it wisely.

Education through the Years

I'm not talking about the history of public or higher education, but rather the way our society grooms children in the name of education from a very young age. Education through the years of our lives starts as early as age two or three in preschool and day care. When I worked at a day care in my early twenties, I was a teacher's assistant in the early preschool room, which had kids who were around three and four years of age and still mastering potty training. And we had lesson plans for these kids, including story time, fine motor and gross motor skills, colors, letters and numbers, etc. It was all very age-appropriate, but you can't force a kid to learn their numbers when they can't stop thinking about playing trains.

A lot of the time, that's what public education felt like to me. Going from class to class, regardless of whether I was in the mood for calculus. Even in grade school, I found myself rushing a weekly reading journal each Sunday night, in tears because I hadn't read and done the journaling each day and was trying to cram it all in. School was about performance and recitation. For the most part, that was fine with me, because I could learn and pick up new information through lecture, note-taking, and review.

Then, in college, when I took Educational Psychology, I learned that there are many ways to process new information and that one size does not fit all. In the mind of an early preschooler, playing and running and collaborating with other kids with blocks *is learning*. Learning isn't about tests or scores or how to diagram a sentence.

This disconnect between practical application and rote recitation is a contributing factor to the rise of homeschooling, Montessori and Waldorf schools, and other alternatives to traditional public schooling.

The National Center for Montessori in the Public Sector reports on four decades of growth in the Montessori school model, with data from 1975–2014.[26] Public Montessori Schools saw steady growth through the 1970s, '80s, and '90s, and then experienced a huge boom of over three hundred new schools opened since 2000. It looks like the Millennials are choosing alternate education for their kids, and the organization notes that the current "wave" of Montessori interest and growth is focused on an alternative to traditional schools.

Homeschooling has also seen a rise since the '90s, according to ongoing research by the National Center for Education Statistics (NCES). Surveyed parents reported reasons for home education including "concern about the school environment, to provide religious or moral instruction, and dissatisfaction with the academic instruction available at other schools."[27] According to NCES data, "the homeschooling rate [grew] from 1.7 percent of the school-aged student population in 1999 to 3.4 percent in 2012." The homeschooling rate in the United States doubled in that thirteen-year span, but what does it mean for Millennials? It's hard to find specific data on the demographics of who is being homeschooled, so we can't know for sure how old each "school age" child was during the survey years. But what we can see is that homeschooling is on the rise, which seems to show that more parents now are homeschooling their children.[28]

The National Home Education Research Institute explores an apparent plateau in US homeschool rates. Remember that the NCES reported a 3.4 percent homeschool rate in 2012, and compare that to the 3.3 percent homeschool rate reported in 2016. Is homeschooling tapering off, or not? Unfortunately, it's not very clear. Response rates to the survey "decreased from 57.6 percent in 2012 to 49.3 percent in 2016." So, unfortunately, we don't have a perfect estimate of the actual homeschool rate in America. We can assume that with a decreased survey response rate and consistent reported homeschool rate that there is unreported growth at play.[29]

I was briefly homeschooled for half of the third grade, when my mother got pissed off at our school system and yanked all four kids out of school. I remember the homeschooling time fondly, because I got to study whatever I wanted.

We had a big map of the United States up on the wall, and each week I would get to pick a new Native American culture to learn about, and I'd go label their territory on the map when I finished the unit in my workbook. I was fascinated by the different cultures and loved getting to know the states at the same time. I also had a board game involving states and their capitals, and I learned fractions with an educational toy. I made up a homemade newspaper that I wrote with blue crayon on notebook paper, drawing the outline of our county's shape on the front page. I carefully wrote out the weather forecast on the top of the page and drew clouds or sunshine or rain to match.

And then my parents started their divorce process, and we got put back into school. I remember asking my teacher if I would pass third grade because I had missed so much of the school year, and she explained to me, a tearful eight-year-old, that I hadn't missed school at all, I had just done it at home. I was having such a good time learning at home that I didn't realize it counted as school. How many other kids could benefit from learning at home in their own way, at their own pace?

The biggest argument against homeschooling, the thing that everyone says after sucking in air through their teeth in a "Hm, I just don't know about that" way, is the concept of socialization. "How will they meet other kids and get along with others? How will they learn how to exist in the world like normal people? You don't want them to be weird homeschool kids, right?" Like homeschooled kids are just locked in a basement with some flash cards and crawl out to graduate high school? Homeschooled kids can go on field trips any day of the week, learn alongside their siblings or peers in co-op groups, and generally don't have trouble making friends.

Also, homeschooled kids get enough sleep. Teenagers need about nine hours of sleep a night. Nine hours! So if they need nine hours to sleep and eight hours for school, that leaves seven hours for homework, eating, extracurricular activities and sports, and relaxing. We start stressing our kids out in middle school or even sooner with schedules like this.

How much socializing are public school students getting that homeschool students aren't? It seems more likely that "socialization" is just a nice-sounding code word for "learning their place in society." The truth is that kids may or may not learn well in public schools, may or may not make friends regardless of where they learn, and may or may not do well on test scores regardless of their intelligence. Tests are a crappy way to measure how smart somebody is, and school is all about testing and funding. It's not really about kids. I say this as someone who did very well in public school and graduated in the top ten percent of her class.

The fact that I did well on my standardized tests doesn't mean anything about how well I do in society or how easily I learn new things. And, unfortunately, when students are all taught in the same way, some students aren't going to do well on tests. Further, when some students don't do well on tests, their school doesn't get as much public funding for programming and investment back into education. This happens disproportionately to inner-city and urban-area schools with a high population of students of color.

Racism in Schools

More and more, white Millennials are popping their bubbles of blissful ignorance and facing up to the ways we've benefitted from systems designed to raise us up and keep others down. According to a 2014 data report from the US Department of Education's Office for Civil Rights, Black children are suspended more frequently and disproportionately than white children in preschool.[30] Did you know that preschoolers get suspended? Seriously, suspended. And it's much more likely to happen to Black preschoolers than white ones. When a child is sent home from preschool, that means Mom or Dad has to be home with them or arrange for other childcare, which means more financial impact on Black families than white families.

This inequality of school suspension unsurprisingly continues throughout students' school careers. Additionally, students with disabilities and those for whom English is a second language are also disproportionately suspended. Black students and students with disabilities have the police called to school more often and are arrested in school more frequently than their white and non-disabled peers. Similarly, students with disabilities and students of color are far more likely to be secluded or confined in school.

Segregation still exists in American society. Not like the images from the 1950s, with white school girls screaming at their new classmates, stories of the white kids throwing rocks at school buses full of Black students, or labeled drinking fountains. But looking at the data, our schools are still segregated in the twenty-first century. So much for post-racial society.

A report from Charlotte-Mecklenburg Schools in February 2018, entitled *Breaking the Link,* explores the link between school demographics and outcomes in the district. Their findings highlight the continuing effects of segregation in public schools. The report found that "for all grade spans, low-poverty schools were composed of mostly white students, whereas in high-poverty schools, the majority of students were Black and Hispanic." They also found that standardized test scores indicating grade level proficiency and career readiness decreased as poverty rates increased. Overall, across the district, close to fifty percent of high school graduates took a college-level course; however, there was a striking disparity between low and high-poverty schools. In high-poverty schools, approximately 25.4 percent of graduates completed a college-level course, while low-poverty schools had a rate of 61.1 percent. Additionally, the pass rates for Advanced Placement tests were about ten times higher in low-poverty schools than high-poverty schools. High-poverty schools also reported more chronic absences and out-of-school suspensions.[31]

There is also a glaring racial disparity in special education intervention. Dr. Jawanza Kunjufu asks, in his book *Keeping Black Boys Out of Special Education:*

> *"Why are African American males placed in special education more than any other group? Why are white females placed in special education the least? Why are white males placed in special education more than white females?...Why is there a lesser chance of a male being placed in special education in Europe than in America? Is there any correlation between the low percentage of white females in special education and the fact that 83 percent of elementary school teachers are white females? Could the reason for the high placement rate of African American males in special education be that African American male teachers count for only 1 percent of all teachers in public schools?"[32]*
>
> *—Dr. Jawanza Kunjufu,* Keeping Black Boys Out of Special Education

Dr. Kunjufu also points out that African American boys are also disproportionately diagnosed with learning disabilities, attention deficit disorders, and developmental disabilities. In his experience, educators and administrators have bent over

backward to justify the alleged reasons for these disparities—
"poverty, environment, and family background." However,
why then is it that there are vastly more Black boys in special
ed than Black girls, who presumably have similar cultural and
environmental backgrounds? Something is amiss. Dr. Kunjufu
refuses the status quo, stating that "the regular classroom is not
culturally sensitive to the needs of this unique population [of
African American boys]."

The American education system is set up to educate the
neurotypical white child first and foremost.

Thanks to these oppressive practices in our education system,
students of color have higher dropout and lower graduation
rates, and thus also have lower college enrollment and graduation
rates than white students. This leaves them even further
behind and highlights the fact that our education system still
has a long way to go since *Brown v. Board of Education*. And
remember—Millennials are a diverse generational cohort who
support policies seeking to improve the position of minorities in
society. We see these problems clearly and we're not looking the
other way.

"Millennials" is no longer synonymous with "kids these days."
The youngest Millennials are now entering college and the oldest
are approaching age forty, with decades in the workforce. And
this generation has exponentially advanced alongside technology
and in a time of social media and political upheaval, amid a
chorus of "Me too" and "Never again."

Emma Gonzalez, of Marjory Stoneman Douglas High School
in Parkland, Florida, was born in 1999, just under the cutoff

to be considered part of this generation's twenty-year cohort. She exemplifies the Millennial spirit to call out problematic behavior and policy, and she became the face of the Parkland school shooting in early 2018. Amid devastation and loss, she and a group of classmates started a grassroots campaign for gun control in the United States. Critics were quick to point out that these damn kids had no place involving themselves in political discourse, a fast and easy way to spread doubt about the Parkland group's relevance and credibility, even though they're approaching voting age and all just survived a school shooting. Seems credible to me.

To make a long story short, society thinks having kids in school is really important and fundamental to their assimilation into adulthood but doesn't take near-adult children seriously when they have opinions that go against the status quo. It's yet another example of the "respect your elders" (which really means "sit down and shut up while the adults are talking") trope.

But then, gloriously, these children grow up. They decide what to do with their lives. Maybe they'll go to college, maybe they won't. Either way, Millennials are coming for the Boomers and we are really tired of you telling us to shut up.

So, You Want to Go to College

College is great, if it's what you want. It is a legitimate and valuable choice. But it's not something you should pursue without a lot of thought. Choose a school you can afford. Not on loans, not based on the median income of people who graduate with your degree, and not based on what your parents think. To pay for school, apply for scholarships and grants, or attend classes part-time while you work and pay cash for school. If your parents are helping you pay, or you have a college fund, look at the total budget and find a school that fits the numbers.

Don't take on massive debt for something that might not work out. What if a family member gets sick and you need to take a temporary leave? Those loans will come due. Or you might decide to take a break from school or completely change career paths, and those loans will follow you.

Be sure to study something *you* care about and that gives you a sense of drive and purpose. If you're only going to college because it's expected of you, or because it's the school your dad attended, or any other reason besides it's what makes you excited as hell, take a step back and think about it. See the recommendations in the next section on taking a year off before school to really learn about yourself.

So, You *Might* Want to Go to College

Contrary to what seems like everyone's behavior and attitude, there's no law that says you have to start college right after high school. Take a year. Take two or three. Travel, get a job, see what the world might hold for you outside the pages of a course catalog or a pamphlet with students laughing on the cover, immortalized in a staged joke. College is great, but you can take your time.

You can also choose to attend part-time, or even audit classes to get an idea of your interests and career aspirations. Community college is an excellent way to try a few areas of study without a hefty price tag.

Please don't worry about being an "older" college student. You're what they call "nontraditional" and trust me, a good college will bend over backward to make sure you feel valued, welcome, and normal. More and more students are starting or returning to college beyond the typical age range of eighteen to twenty-two. You're in good company.

So, You *Don't* Want to Go to College

Many successful people either dropped out or never attended in the first place, and they did just fine. If college isn't in your plans, consider shadowing, apprenticing, or taking local career center or community college classes for vocational training. Skilled work that doesn't require a degree is just as valuable as degree-related work.

The following average hourly rates are taken from the US Bureau of Labor Statistics May 2017 estimates, according to trade-schools.net, which lists several other top-paying trade school jobs.[33]

Construction Manager: $48.56
Boilermaker: $30.30
Aircraft Mechanic: $30.07
Plumber: $27.44
Electrician: $27.84
Crane Operator: $26.78
CNC Machine Tool Programmer: $26.81

HVAC Technician: $24.95
Welder: $20.87

Or, if you're entrepreneurial, you can even start your own business. Attend local think tank or mastermind groups, or even check out your local library's ongoing classes and group sessions to meet other people who have great ideas. Read books, attend seminars, or join online academies designed to help you turn your ideas into a real business. Whatever dream you have, make a plan and go for it.

While you're at it, don't let anybody shame you for not going to college. Living your authentic life is worth way more than a degree saddled with five-figure student loan debt.

How to Make Sure You're Killing It

Whether you go to college at eighteen, twenty-five, or never, you can be successful in your chosen career. Just make your choice with purpose, and always keep an open mind. You may decide after twenty years as an entrepreneur to go for a degree in a new field, for the first time in your life. You may collect degree after degree as you realize you're a super-educated jack of all trades. Or you may fall somewhere in the middle. And that's fine, as long as you're living your life authentically.

Follow your passion. If you know in high school what your interests and passions are, by all means, follow them to college. If you're not sure, but you still know you want to go to college, go and kick around a few elective classes to see if something pops out at you. Don't be afraid to take some time off and try different jobs or skills out to see what really makes you feel awesome.

Work feels like work. The adage, "If you do what you love, you'll never work a day in your life" is not necessarily true. No matter what career path you decide on, there will be some days when work is boring, or work is hard, or work is annoying. That's not a reason to throw in the towel and change jobs or majors or career paths, but if you start feeling like your career is deeply wrong for you, it's time to make a change.

It's never too late. If you didn't go to college in your twenties, it's not too late. If you're in your forties and want to make a career change, it's not too late. Nothing is ever too late when it comes to living a life that makes you happy—as long as you can make those changes reasonably, without putting your finances or family in jeopardy.

Avoid debt. As much as possible, avoid going into debt for school or career (or any reason). Choose a school you can afford with cash while working, or look into scholarships and grants, which are available for nearly every interest or skill.

There are other options than college. Technical training schools and community colleges are great for specialized training to succeed without a four-year degree. Check out your local associate degree programs to dip your toe into a new skill or course of study.

Choose a major wisely. Pick a major or course of study that will provide the best education for you to have options later; don't pigeonhole yourself into one type of career choice. For instance,

English majors can leverage their educational background as creative writers, performers, journalists, etc. (PS: My degrees are in psychology and higher education, and I ended up full-time in marketing, so anything's possible.)

Start your own gig. Starting your own business is possible without the need for high-dollar startup capital. Again, avoid going into debt to start a business. Start small while you're doing something else to pay the bills, and you can grow your business organically over time without risking it all. Consider online educational tools like Lynda.com and Udemy, podcasts like Pat Flynn's Smart Passive Income and Harvard Business Review's HBR IdeaCast, and books such as *Rich20Something* by Daniel DiPiazza and *Grit* by Angela Duckworth.

Part II

Millennials Are Destroying Society

Chapter 5

Millennials Are Killing Diet and Fitness

"Millennials are killing a $1 billion diet staple"

—Business Insider, September 2016

"Millennials more likely to ditch diet mentality"

—Food Business News, November 2015

"Millennials are killing gyms, too"

—*New York Post*, October 2016

"How Millennials Ended the Running Boom"

—*Wall Street Journal*, May 2016

As a marketing professional, I savor the moments when I feel bested by the clear and deliberate manipulations of advertising. If something is in green packaging with leaves on it, I will immediately pick it up and see if it's actually eco-friendly or just greenwashed to appeal to my inner earth goddess. If it's legit, I learn about a new brand. If it's hot air, I place it back on the shelf with a wag of my finger, letting it know it hasn't fooled me. So, when I was scrolling through Facebook one day and saw an advertisement for a weight-loss app for Millennials, I clicked on it. I have a vested interest in all things Millennial, of course.

Turns out the app, called Noom, is a weight-loss app for smartphones that is geared toward overall lifestyle and behavior change, including a food diary and exercise log, similar to most weight loss apps. The difference with Noom, however, is that it also includes coaching, support, tips for handling common weight-loss fears and anxieties, and a method to track binge-eating triggers. They even have a diabetes prevention program.

This chapter isn't an advertisement for Noom. I didn't sign up to try it, so I can't talk about its success. However, I have used a handful of habit and fitness tracking apps over the last decade, including MapMyRun, MyFitnessPal, HabitShare, Aaptiv, Charity Miles, Fitbit, Strava, and My Water (stay hydrated, friends). I've been in online weight-loss groups. I've done the MLM shakes. I've done the home workouts. I've done the diets, including low-fat, low-carb, paleo, gluten-free, and more.

But given the overwhelming media jabs at Millennials for destroying diet and fitness, I can't help but wonder why and how we're doing so.

My Weight-Loss Journey

My weight-loss journey (and, to be totally honest, my fucked-up relationship with food and my immense shame in my body) began when I was a child. I was raised on a steady diet of "You eat like a pig," "No man will want to date you if you eat like that," "You're fat," and my mother's all-time greatest hit, "Okay, it's your body," recited in a singsong voice when my sister or I would ask for a Little Debbie snack or a popsicle.

Food was punishment. Food was reward. Food was a battlefield. We'd be dropped off at the babysitter's with a list of dietary restrictions, including how much meat, dairy, and grains we were to eat each day, which the babysitter promptly ignored as she directed us to the basement freezer for an ice cream. Our dad, ever the buddy parent, let us eat ice cream for dinner when we weren't living off Tyson teriyaki chicken breasts and Knorr rice sides. Thus, my middle and high school years were plagued with overeating, hiding my consumption of sugar, and generally being the shy but funny, and definitely smart, fat girl in every teenage drama.

Exercise was hit-or-miss as well (which is a fairly accurate representation of kickball, which I hated because I am not a fast person). Throughout my entire public school career, I learned to fake injuries to get out of PE classes. I felt embarrassed to have to try sports in gym, mortified when the teams got picked, and filled with an ongoing sense of dread for any physical activity where people could see me. When running the mile in high school, I commented to a friend that I had nearly thrown up, and she said, "Why? You weren't even running fast." When I actually had a genuine interest in the new field hockey team forming at my school, my mom talked me out of it because she didn't want to spend the money on equipment if I wasn't sure I'd like it (code for if I decided to quit).

As depression and anxiety took hold over the years, my weight ballooned. Finally, in a Planned Parenthood in Akron, Ohio, where I got my annual pelvic exam and birth control prescription because I was broke as hell, the nurse had to ka-chunk that counterweight on the scale over another fifty pounds, confirming that I had topped out at three hundred pounds exactly. I was devastated.

I lost twenty pounds by eating more veggies, drinking more water, and borrowing *Fat Burning Workout for Dummies* from the library. I have watched my weight yo-yo up and down over the intervening decade, but I've also made incredible progress on my lifestyle and am the healthiest I've ever been, despite my BMI.

I eat about 90 percent vegan, save for the occasional honey or (gasp) backyard chicken eggs from local farmers. I focus on whole foods (did you know Oreo cookies are vegan? It's true. Vegan does not equal healthy). I don't stress out about macros. I track my calories, sometimes. I don't love greens, but I am working on learning to enjoy them (or at least eat them without gagging). I drink plenty of water.

And it turns out that I really, really love exercise. I run, I bike, I swim, I lift weights, I do kickboxing. I'm learning calisthenics, and by the time this book is published, I may have finally been able to do one single pull-up. I've run two half marathons and countless 5k and 10k races. I've done a Ragnar race. This body can work.

And it doesn't need any diet yogurt. Has anyone stopped to consider that food trends change as more research is done on food? It's proven that a low-fat diet is absolute bananas. Low fat typically means full of chemicals, sugar, and salt to get it to taste like not-garbage. Fun yogurt commercials aside (they are soooo good), the market has spoken, and the market says, "Down with shitty low-fat food!"

The Timely Deaths of Diets and Gyms

Why exactly do these industries expect us to keep eating nonsense? When news hit the mainstream media that the sugar industry had influenced sub-par research encouraging people to go low-fat, suddenly society as a whole was looking at fat through new eyes. It turns out fat itself is not the demon it was made out to be. In fact, our bodies need healthy fats to run most effectively. Boo hoo, diet yogurt.

Diets are mostly marketing gimmicks and feel more like advertising and product placement than anything designed to help improve your life. I recently saw a magazine cover advertising a diet that would allow you to drop twenty-two pounds in a week. I joked with the cashier that it must be a diet that includes sawing off your leg.

Millennials, having grown up during an enormous media and technology boom with omnipresent advertising, are largely able to ignore ads and claims—especially if they are unable to substantiate them. Like my tale of giving a green, leafy bottle of kitchen cleaner a once-over to determine its legitimacy, Millennials can simply whip out a trusty smartphone or tablet to quickly research any brand in an instant. Some say that we're immune to advertising, but the fact is that we'll click anything to learn more. We may not end up buying it, but there's a decent chance we'll give it a shot if it's a legitimate product.

However, we are able more and more to ignore body-shaming, miracle-promising products. We are skeptical enough to want research and reviews before trying a magic pill, and we increasingly demand to see real people instead of photoshopped thin bodies. Body positivity goes a long way toward advertising to Millennials. I once bought workout pants off Target's website based solely on the fact that they used an actual plus-sized athlete in their ads. So, we're not actually immune to ads, we just want ads for real things.

As a culture, we're obsessed with weight loss, beach bodies, losing the baby weight, putting plastic wrap around our tummies, and taking pills to promote a higher metabolism. But you don't need a special Low-Carb High-Protein All-Grass-Fed Non-GMO Defatted Peanut Butter granola bar with 100 percent real tree bark to eat healthfully. Despite being raised by diet-crazed mothers who used to Sweat to the Oldies, the Millennials are figuring out that maybe if we just, like, eat some real food and move a little bit, things will work out okay.

Oh, also—we remember Physical Education class. For those of us who weren't super into group fitness in our youth, PE was a nightmare. So, any fitness routine that puts us back in that mental state is a hard thing to overcome, whether it's a weight room or running on a track or participating in a class or even doing a push-up. To this day, I cannot do a push-up without thinking of my ninth-grade push-up test and how I just gave up so I wouldn't have to struggle and feel further embarrassed.

Millennials are indeed working out, but we tend to eschew the traditional gym. When it comes to "killing the gym," the latest trend is a pay-as-you-go studio experience. Those overworked, chronically busy, gotta-hustle Millennials sometimes can't make it to the gym consistently and resent having to pay a monthly fee or be locked into a contract. Instead, they opt for classes with a drop-in fee they can attend as their schedule allows, or something more flexible that they can pause and pick back up as needed. Plus, Millennials and the younger Gen Z prefer to spend their money on small businesses and brands rather than large chains, especially as they move up the income ladder and want to make more of an investment in their health than whatever local gym is the cheapest.

Fitness studios offer smaller classes, more individual attention, and a sense of community that Millennials thrive on. We want to feel like individuals, not just a barcode that scans in, pounds out some reps, and then leaves to rinse and repeat the next day. Having to sign up for a class and knowing there will only be eight or ten people in it feels a little more special, and it doesn't leave us feeling embarrassed or worried about hiding in the back of the room. A smaller group feels inherently more welcoming, and the instructors tend to connect on an individual level with participants.

Another popular trend in fitness is on-demand workout streaming services that allow people to work out at home, on their own timetable. Guided workout apps for smartphones are also booming, offering workouts to popular music in a variety of intensities and lengths—perfect for a busy Millennial who needs to get in a quick run on lunch or get into a ten-minute stretch and strength routine in the mornings before work.

The popular boutique experience isn't necessarily cheaper than a gym membership and is sometimes astronomically higher, but for many Millennial adults, it's well worth it to feel like they're making an investment they can control, and which helps their mental health as well.

The Link Between Physical and Mental Health

You know the internet meme with a misty forest, or a pair of laced-up running shoes, emblazoned with the caption, "This is an antidepressant," contrasted with an image of pills that says, "This is shit"? Falsehoods.

Yes, there's obviously a link between physical activity and mental health. Movement makes endorphins. Endorphins make you happy. But if you can't make your own neurotransmitters, store-bought is fine. Research indicates that exercise can indeed benefit those who have clinical depression and anxiety disorders, but it's not going to completely replace medication and therapy for most patients.

According to an article published by the American Psychological Association, moderate exercise typically results in a better mood within five minutes, and research indicates that exercise can also help to reduce the effects of depression on a long-term basis. Additionally, regular exercise has also been shown to reduce anxiety and panic disorders by exposing the body to increased heart rate, perspiration, and stress in a controlled way (exercise) as opposed to an uncontrollable anxiety or panic attack. While these studies and results are promising, there is still much work to be done in identifying the best types of exercise that mental health professionals should recommend as part of ongoing treatment plans (Weir, 2011).

Unfortunately, not everyone who would theoretically benefit from regular exercise is able to do so. People with mobility issues, joint pain, or other physical challenges can't always lace up a pair of shoes and go out for a morning jog. Plus, they're getting really tired of people asking them if they've tried yoga yet. They've probably tried yoga.

There's also the Catch-22 that, while exercise can help improve the symptoms and recovery of depression, anxiety, and other mood disorders, sometimes it's kind of hard to get out the door to go for a walk or hit the gym if you're smack in the middle of a depressive episode. However, this is often the time when exercise would benefit people with depression the most, since just a small amount of exercise can help to boost mood.

The Obesity Epidemic in America

So…what's up with all these overweight Millennials who hate diet yogurt and gym memberships? Let's explore some of the root causes of the so-called obesity epidemic in the United States.

Overall, Americans are eating more processed food, including trans fats, sugar and refined carbohydrates, and artificial dyes, preservatives, and sweeteners. We're moving less and lead a more sedentary lifestyle than previous generations. We're not sleeping as much, which leads to a lack of energy to exercise and prompts us to reach for quick sugar fixes, caffeine all day long, and easy processed foods because honestly, who wants to cook when you're this tired? Have some cereal (oh wait, Business Insider says "Millennials aren't eating cereal because it's too much work").

American society has adopted the trend of immediate gratification. You can order anything you could possibly need online and have it delivered to your door in a matter of days, so we barely have to leave the house. While this is a literal lifesaver for people in poverty or with mobility issues, chronic pain, other disabilities, transportation challenges, etc., the average consumer can simply window-shop at their leisure, accidentally kill hours of their day, and then go to bed groggy from staring at a screen all day, only to have interrupted sleep and Amazon Prime fever dreams. This does not a healthy cycle make.

Speaking of poverty, disability, etc., it's important to address the concept of food deserts and the energy and ability levels required to prepare fresh foods. Not every city or state has access to affordable, fresh, whole foods. Sometimes it's a decision between processed snacks or nothing. While we're at it, let's agree to stop sticking our noses in the business of people who receive food stamps and other benefits, shall we? Additionally, for people with chronic pain or mobility issues, sometimes standing up to cook, chopping vegetables with a knife, or holding a heavy pot of water are simply too painful to bear. We cannot force people to consume a certain way when there is such a vast spectrum of incomes, abilities, and even grocery availability throughout the country.

Convenience Foods of the Future

A chapter on diet and food wouldn't be complete without mentioning the online shopping experience that is food subscription plans. Whether you want complete meals or a sampling of snacks, no matter your dietary restrictions—vegan, paleo, gluten-free, or anything else—there is a subscription service for you. It's not exactly flying cars, but it's safe to say the future has arrived. Now that semi-prepped and packaged meals can be delivered to your door in refrigerated packaging so all you have to do is follow a recipe. Although, I know Meals on Wheels exists, so it's not like meal delivery is a totally new thing. Getting to customize your order is pretty cool, though.

There are also online food shops, like Brandless and Thrive Market, which allow you to shop at a considerable discount because of lower overhead costs than your typical store. Thrive Market also donates a membership to a family in need for each paid membership (about sixty dollars a year, similar to large warehouse stores). If there's one thing Millennials love more than small, local businesses, it's socially conscious brands that offer discounts and convenience.

Until we figure out Replicator technology (think Star Trek, not Stargate), getting a monthly or weekly box of food seems rather futuristic and exciting.

How to Make Sure You're Killing It

Call Out the Status Quo. When you see a magazine cover, an Instagram ad, or even a body-shaming "joke" made by a friend, call it out. We need to silence body shaming as soon as it happens. It doesn't matter if you're a killjoy; someone who has experienced guilt or shame about their body will appreciate the moment it takes you to call out someone's inappropriate behavior. In classic Millennial fashion, tag brands on social media to demand answers about why they photoshop models, how they once again failed to acknowledge Black skin tones in their ads, or why the fat girl models are all in "modest" clothes. Ask questions. Normalize all bodies.

Add A Little BoPo (Body Positivity). Screw the diet mentality and its built-in body shaming. Understand that your body is where you live, and nothing about that is shameful. Celebrate your wins in wellness, whether that means you're excited to lose five pounds or excited to finally have a day where you had the energy to get out of bed and wash a few dishes. Your brain is part of your body, and it's okay to celebrate a day when you won a battle in your brain. Body positivity is for all parts of you. While we're sprinkling around the self-love, share that newfound confidence with your friends and loved ones, too. Tell them they look great, without congratulating on weight loss.

Eat the Tasty Food. Life is too short to make yourself choke down a salad if you hate raw veggies or eat unseasoned boiled food in the name of losing weight. If it's someone's birthday, have a slice of cake. If you're at a brunch, it's okay to have an extra glass of that tasty pineapple juice. Food fuels our body, but it can also bring pleasure, and that's okay. Aim to eat mostly plants, whole food carbohydrates, moderate protein, and some healthy fats (avocado, of course!).

Hydrate. Aim to drink water at a rate of half your body weight in ounces per day. If you weigh 180 pounds, drink ninety ounces of water. Sparkling counts. Soda doesn't. Yes, you will pee a lot.

Get Enough Sleep. I'm ranking sleep as more important than exercise for a reason. If you're not getting enough sleep, you will run at a deficit and risk injury due to fatigue during your workouts. Plus, you just feel like crap when you can't sleep. Knock off the screen time one to two hours before bed, and commit to at least six hours a night, though some people may thrive more on up to nine hours. Sleep cycles average around ninety minutes, so aim for either six, seven and a half, or nine full hours of sleep, so you're not waking up in the middle of a cycle. Be in bed by ten thirty.

Move Your Body. Whether it's a good stretch a few times a day, a short bodyweight workout, running, cardio DVDs, or anything else, getting activity during the day helps your overall physical and mental health, and it can also help you avoid paying for a gym membership, since we're killing those now. Even going for a leisurely walk will help boost your mood, even when (or especially when) you just don't feel like going. Regular exercise also helps you develop a healthy sleep cycle.

Find a Buddy. Try searching for local fitness groups, or even large online wellness communities. They have so many members, you're bound to find someone local who wants to have a meal prep party or go for a bike ride around the local trails. I actually found a workout buddy in a Harry Potter-themed running community on Facebook. If meeting strangers from the internet isn't your style, look up local running groups and go meet a whole bunch of strangers at once!

Reduce Caffeine. *Gasp!* Yes, sadly, caffeine can be to blame for insomnia, restlessness, and funky heart rate. Your morning cup or two are probably fine, but watch out for the midday slump and evening pick-me-up, when you'll be tempted to grab a late cup of something to rouse you.

Evaluate Your Budget. Be real with your finances and figure out how much you can devote to groceries each month. Fresh, organic produce and cute expensive things in mason jars are great, but they aren't necessary to live. Feed yourself and your family, but make sure food isn't taking over your life or your finances.

Focus on Habits. You don't have to change your lifestyle overnight. Focus on building small, healthy habits, like drinking a glass of water before your morning coffee, or snacking on fruit at night instead of a cookie. One of my favorite habits to build is only eating a sweet treat if I made it myself. If I'm in the mood to eat cake, I better also be in the mood to bake it.

Don't Get Hung Up on the Numbers. The scale is the biggest liar you'll ever meet, and this is a book about gaslighting. The scale reports one piece of information: How hard is gravity sucking your mass toward Earth's core? You could lose weight by going to the moon, because there would be less gravity sucking your mass downward (very scientific, I know). When it comes to measuring your wellness success, don't get hung up on the scale numbers. Take body measurements and photos. Do fitness tests that count how many squats, pushups, and jumping jacks you can do in a minute, and track the results over time. Get your body fat percentage evaluated and track the progress.

Celebrate the Non-Scale Victories. Related to the above point, noticing and acknowledging the non-scale victories has so much power. My boyfriend and I realized at the gym the other week that, even though I'm fat and slow, my endurance running habits have paid off. I was able to out-squat him by over fifty pounds. Girl has legs!

Try Yoga. Really, though. Have you tried yoga?

Chapter 6

Millennials Are Killing the Economy

"Millennials are killing the movie business"

—New York Post, April 2016

"Why aren't Millennials buying diamonds?"

—The Economist, June 2016

I t really all boils down to this one, right? Millennials are destroying industries and products left and right, personally responsible for the demise of Applebee's, paper napkins, low-fat dairy products, dieting, and plastic straws. This blatant and ubiquitous finger-pointing is one more attempt to accuse us of ruining the fun for everyone else, despite the fact that industries change over time and maybe your product has simply reached the end of its time to shine. Do you see Apple out there whining that nobody buys an iPod Shuffle anymore? Hell no! Apple gets with the times and offers new, better, on-trend offerings. And when we've all got our cell phones directly embedded into our brains or our forearms or whatever the future holds, they'll come up with something else.

Did Millennials destroy huge tube television sets, or did technology improve to the point where flat screens are accessible and affordable? Did Millennials destroy desktop computers, or have developments in laptops and tablets offer a more realistic solution for people to take their work on the go? Did we destroy USB drives, or did Google and Apple perfect cloud technology?

Why is it so much easier to point at a whole generation of young adults and say, "Oh my God, they killed JC Penney" than it is to realistically grasp the concept that technology and societal needs change over time? For each thing "destroyed" by Millennials, take a look around and see if something else has developed in its place.

We're killing restaurants but giving rise to meal subscription services. We're killing grocery store chains while promoting low-overhead online alternatives like Thrive Market and Brandless.

We're killing diamonds and jewelers instead supporting a robust network of Etsy sellers who offer their handmade wares from across the globe. We're killing the housing industry but really adding to Pinterest's archive of avocado toast recipes (I am never going to stop making this joke, ever).

What does this mean, for consumerism, for capitalism, and for the economy at large? Are Millennials wielding their mighty collective Twitter presence to destroy the way we buy things and exchange money for goods and services? You betcha.

Ethical Consumption

Here's one of the internet's favorite phrases these days: There is no ethical consumption under capitalism. You may be surprised to note, after consuming this book about how I think society needs to sit down and think about what it has done, that I'm not anti-capitalist. Capitalism at its core simply means exchanging something for something else. When I buy handmade jewelry or home decor items from a seller online, I'm participating in capitalism. Supporting a work-at-home mom in her home business is capitalism. Grabbing a salad at your local organic cafe is capitalism. Capitalism is a free market exchange of goods and services.

The problem with capitalism isn't the concept itself, but the way society has let large corporations off the hook for accountability; for example, companies often destroy overstock rather than allowing it to be consumed without profit, and industry takes a major toll on the environment without needing to take responsibility. The problem with capitalism is regulations that simultaneously allow mega-corporations to skirt accountability for harm they do while punishing small businesses and individuals with fines and fees and red tape when they're trying to make a buck to live.

Millennials aren't out to destroy capitalism or big-box stores, we're not trying to take society back to the barter system (although we *do* barter), and we don't want to overthrow the government (well, maybe a little bit). We just want to know what a business is doing, how it operates, and whether its executives do their best to not leave the earth a sad wreck. But if companies insist on hiding behind regulations, tax shelters, and exorbitant CEO salaries, the Millennials aren't here for it.

The message is simple: Do better or get lost.

The Minsumer Phenomenon

When I first started blogging in 2012, I had been following several minimalist blogs, which inspired my start as a lifestyle minimalism writer. Think *The Life-Changing Magic of Tidying Up*, but with slightly less whimsy. In my journey down the minimalist blogosphere rabbit hole, I learned about the term "minsumerism," which basically means reducing your retail footprint. Upcycle or repurpose things, shop secondhand, and try to reduce packaging waste and buying stuff just for stuff's sake.

Millennials are living in apartments or smaller homes longer, sometimes living with roommates, or even moving cross-country to take a new job offer, since we all hate our parents and can't wait to leave town. So, it makes sense that we can't just accumulate stuff, because who knows if we'll have the space for it or want to deal with packing it next time we move. Plus, we need money for things like groceries and electricity and new tires and medical bills. We can't hit up the dollar section at Target every day.

People buy and keep stuff for several reasons. They think it will make them feel happy, or safe, or cool. We buy things to impress other people, to make promises to ourselves that we'll lose the weight or finish the project or pick up this cool new hobby, and to feel a sense of control over our environment when we are desperately aware that we don't have our shit together. But no matter what the indulgence is, at some point or another, we tend to look around and think, "Why do I have all this stuff?" It has happened to me twice now, both major purges preceded by a divorce. When I was moving out of my second husband's home, I found a few boxes of things I hadn't even unpacked from when I moved in *four years earlier.* I was also astonished at the fact that I could hardly tell anything had changed as I went through the house packing up rooms. He was such a collector that my things had barely taken up any space.

Because I was so used to taking up small spaces, keeping my belongings in boxes and bins, carving out the smallest areas on shelves to display the things I loved, I was looking at studio apartments and small one-bedroom places when I moved out. It took several friends telling me that I was allowed to take up space before I ended up with a modest two-bedroom apartment in an area I loved. I turned the spare room into a combination art studio, office, and reading nook. Do I go into that room? No, I do not. Do I appreciate having it? Yes, it was part of my process as I left a bad marriage. But I'm still wired as a minimalist and enjoy the creative challenges of making a space that makes me feel happy without filling up with a bunch of stuff for stuff's sake.

We, as a society, simply cannot handle the level of consumption being promoted and sold to us. And, as someone who works in marketing full-time, I can assure you that making you think you absolutely *need* an item in order to live your best life is part of my job. That might sound a little weird, but that's what marketing and sales is all about. That's what capitalism is about. You make a product, and if people want the product, they buy the product. You must tell them what makes your product different or better than the competition, because hoo-boy, in 2019, there is competition everywhere.

I've carefully steered my career trajectory through industries and brands that make me feel good about promoting them, and I'm aware that I am extremely privileged to do so. Not everyone can pick and choose from what jobs are available in their area, let alone the salary and benefits that come with them. But I could, and I've worked in the organic and natural products industries since getting into marketing, because it's important to me to authentically speak highly of the product I'm trying to sell people.

I have worked to achieve a level of quality in how I live my life and represent myself professionally, which has allowed me to continue raising the bar for the quantity of dollars I receive in exchange for my services. Capitalism on a basic level. The more I move up in my career, the more companies are willing to pay for me. When you're job-seeking, you're the product you're selling. Your personality, charisma, expertise, education, and other attributes are your unique selling points, your features and benefits. And you have to have something extra to offer in order to make the sale and get the offer.

Unfortunately, minimum wage isn't a livable wage in most (if not all) of our country, and entry-level employees are treated like plastic forks. If they're not working perfectly, just throw them out and get a new one that doesn't bend funny. But people aren't tools. People aren't objects. People aren't pieces and parts of a grand machine. People are, well, people. And if we're in a capitalist society, these people need money to live. Money means shelter, food, clothing, necessities. Money means life.

And for some ridiculous reason, the people who have money believe that the people who don't have money are out to get their money. For the love, y'all. This has been done time and time again across literature, movies, television, and more. While the peasants are fighting over who has more and building fences to protect their little bit, the rich are up in their castles dabbing red wine off their lips with silk napkins and laughing haughtily.

Capitalism isn't broken, but greed has broken us. And, as a result, we're broke.

The Billionaire Elephant in the Room

According to *Forbes*, the world has over 2,200 billionaires, and over 630 of them live in the United States. Many American billionaires are household names: Michael Bloomberg, the Koch brothers, Mark Zuckerberg, Warren Buffett, Jeff Bezos, Bill Gates, Oprah, the Waltons, Elon Musk, and the list goes on.

Quick question, though: who the hell needs so much money?

In a 2009 report, published by the Indiana Business Research Center at Indiana University's Kelley School of Business, researchers investigated census data to project lifetime earnings based on degree level. On average, someone with a bachelor's degree or higher can expect to earn a cumulative $1.8 million in their lifetime. Of course, this is an average breakdown across sexes; when broken down by sex, men will earn an estimated $2.1 million for the average woman's $1.4 million. Even men with a high school diploma can expect to cross the million-dollar lifetime threshold. This data reflects cumulative gross income and does not necessarily reflect the amount of money someone will have at retirement.

All this is to say, a billionaire isn't just an extra super millionaire. One billion dollars is one thousand millions. A person who has a billion dollars has the lifetime earnings of one thousand average high school graduates.

The net worth of Jeff Bezos is $159.2 billion. That is equal to the lifetime earnings of the entire population of Eugene, Oregon (assuming every one of Eugene's 160,000+ residents boasts a high school diploma). The net worth of Jeff Bezos is equal to over 360 LeBron Jameses or 350 Beyoncés. Meanwhile, in July 2018, a worker strike among Amazon employees in Spain and Germany made a dent in Prime Day sales as a protest for better working conditions, pay, and benefits. In an August 2018 article by Business Insider, Amazon was found to have an average 10 percent of its employees in Pennsylvania and Ohio on food-stamp benefits.

The Walton family had a combined net worth of about $140 billion in 2017, while Wal-Mart is constantly under the media microscope for having so many workers on public assistance to make ends meet. Despite announcing a two-dollar wage increase for its Ohio stores in January 2018, over 11,500 Ohio employees were found to be on public assistance.

The list goes on and on. Brands with billions don't pay enough to their workers for basic living wages, and somehow society manages to point the blame at avocado toast instead of corporate greed. Can we pull back for a second and take a look at the bigger picture?

I don't know how to fix this problem. I am not a financial analyst or an expert on corporate taxes or government assistance. But I can tell you that it is not Millennials' fault.

Poverty and the Benefits Gap

It behooves the upper crust of society to have us all fighting with each other, spitting slurs at the mom with a benefits card in the grocery checkout, or shooting dirty looks at someone pregnant with four kids already. "Don't you know what causes that? I can't believe my tax dollars go to buy your kids candy, ice cream, and—is that steak? How dare you." As if people in poverty deserve no indulgences.

For all the jokes about lattes and avocados, the truth is that Millennials are broke. We're poor. We're impoverished. We don't have a lot of dough. Reported by Fox Business in 2017, a study based on Pew Research Center data showed that 5.3 million

United States households living below the poverty line are
Millennials. Baby Boomers made up 5 million, and Generation
X came in at 4.2 million, of approximately 17 million total
households.[34]

As such, no, we're not buying houses. We're not buying
diamonds. We're barely buying food. The same research reported
that "Millennial heads of households were more likely than
previous generations to be minorities and/or unmarried." Not
participating in white hetero-marriage culture means a higher
rate of poverty. And, as if you didn't know this when writing your
monthly check to your landlord, Millennials are also more likely
to rent instead of owning their home.

We're also seeing an increase of over 450 percent in student loan
balances since 2003. All our money is going to keeping a roof
over our head and our loans out of forbearance, but tell me again
how Millennials are so lazy and entitled. Who deserves your
grumbles about tax dollars and benefits? The single mom with
two jobs who dares to need help buying her groceries? Or the guy
who literally bought a grocery chain because he could?

As people point the finger at those who receive government
assistance, whether it's food stamps, Medicare, day care
assistance, disability, or anything else, it's important to know the
tenuous line that those on benefits must walk. It's not as simple
as being poor, applying, and getting your benefits in the mail.
People on assistance must be poor enough to qualify, with an
income at or below varying levels of the poverty line, but if they
get a raise at work, they could be disqualified for their benefits
and end up even more broke than before.

This phenomenon is known as the benefits gap, or benefits cliff. A raise as relatively low as fifty cents per hour could lose a family their food assistance, leaving them worse off than before they got their raise. Without a living wage, those in poverty will continue to fall further behind.

Additionally, our society also has the unfortunate habit of judging people's worth based on the amount of money and work they can produce. Employees with disabilities, mental or physical, are expected to perform at the same level as their able counterparts and must jump through hoop after hoop to receive accommodations without risking their employment.

Lane, twenty-six, is a special education intervention specialist and teacher in a major metropolitan area in the United States. She has complex post-traumatic stress disorder (C-PTSD), panic disorder, generalized anxiety, and depression. And her mental illness has cost her several jobs throughout adulthood, from part-time college jobs to her full-time career as an educator. Whenever she has asked administrators to provide reasonable accommodations, she is met with an unwillingness to make exceptions to the level of work expected from teachers. That is to say, she's expected to complete her planning work in her off hours, since she doesn't have enough planning time during her workday.

A quick search for "teacher workloads" reveals a disturbing trend of substantiating headlines and excerpts: Teacher workload unmanageable, reducing teacher workload, how unsustainable workloads are destroying the quality of teaching, the dangers of expanding teacher workloads, teacher workloads taking heavy toll, and so on. It's less and less possible to provide accommodations for different types of learners when the administration focuses on test scores as benchmarks of success.

I can hear it now: the dull roar of "But that's not a Millennial problem, ALL teachers have to do that much work." And I completely agree with you. But it's not Lane's fault our education system doesn't support teachers. It's not an issue of entitled and lazy Millennials demanding something different because we're special snowflakes. This has been a problem for decades and we're finally the ones saying "Whoa, this is kind of fucked-up."

People are inherently worthy of respect, love, and support. Regardless of how much they can contribute in an eight-hour workday. Regardless of how much revenue they can generate. Regardless of how well they can pass as normal in a society that demands results and dollar bills to prove how good you are.

Bartering and Millennial Community

Out of the blue, I got a text from a friend asking if she could borrow forty bucks for gas to evacuate coastal North Carolina in the face of Hurricane Florence. A couple weeks before that, a friend asked me to borrow three hundred dollars because her ex-husband hadn't paid his share of their home repair bills she needed to handle to get her house on the market, and she was behind. These friends are college-educated, employed, functional people. And they're broke.

For the record, I gave them both the money and told them I didn't expect it back. Giving charitably is part of how I organize my budget, and it's important to me because the vast majority of my functional, educated, and working friends are so frequently hard up for cash. And it's not a one-too-many-coffees problem. The friend who needed the gas money got a raise at work and fell into the benefits cliff, falling deeper into poverty after the boost in income got her family kicked off benefits that helped pay for food and child care.

I buy from my work-at-home friends, I donate to charity auctions to raise funds, and I support their crowdfunding efforts to keep the electricity on in their homes or replace a broken air conditioner in the middle of summer. Whenever I see a call to action on a fundraising page, I check to see if I've got money to spare. Because when I need people, people show up for me.

I'm privileged to have a good salary and a stable career, but I've been in need too. When I was leaving my husband, I rapidly sold off clothing and baby supplies on my Facebook page, just for the spare cash to buy the basics for my new apartment. I had the deposit and rent saved up, but I forgot I needed things like dishes and sheets and a whole new set of supplies for my cat. Local friends helped me pack and move. One friend even sent me a card with fifty bucks cash in it, with instructions to only spend it on myself, something I wanted but never let myself buy. I bought face wash, a foaming mask, and bubble bath at Target and had a self-care night. Even though I was alone in a new place, I felt supported. Because that is what we do.

When I needed a logo made for a business I was launching, I reached out to a designer friend. I did her resume and a cover letter in exchange for the design work. I also provided blogs and website content for a friend who taught me a childbirth course, so I could be a local friend's doula when she had her third child. Another time, I provided social media content in exchange for coaching to help me write this book. The examples go on and on.

We barter and trade, we show up for each other, and we give each other the space to vent about our struggles. Millennials, you're not making it up. You have it harder than your elders did. And keeping the societal status quo afloat is not your job.

How to Make Sure You're Killing It

Vote with your dollars. So overdone, I know, but it's true! Rather than lament about how shitty Amazon's working conditions are while you rip open your third Prime package of the week, go slightly out of your way to shop somewhere with better policies. Nothing is perfect, but you can detach yourself from the now-now-now of two-day shipping. And buy from brands you believe in. This is what they're afraid of: that we'll stop buying crap. So stop buying the crap! Buy crap with better values.

Don't beat yourself up. If shopping online affords you the ability to handle your household's needs without leaving the house due to physical ability, mental health, lack of transportation, or any other reason that prevents you from getting out, shop online. No one is going to begrudge you getting your needs met without putting yourself in harm's way. Well, if they do, send them to me. But for all us non-disabled people who can handle a trip to Target on our lunch break, let's try that, instead of making some poor soul in an Amazon warehouse run around and pee in a bottle because they're not allowed bathroom breaks.

Reduce consumption. Nothing makes the rich people more annoyed than when you don't buy stuff! Think of what we could do if everyone just bought 10 percent less stuff. Shop secondhand, trade and barter with your friends, make do with what you have…you feel more free when you're not constantly jonesing for something to spend money on. That's your money! You're in charge of where it goes!

Credit scores are not that important. Your credit score is just a measure of how well you interact with your debt. People tell you that you need credit to get anything—a car, a house, an avocado (heh heh), but a pile of cash works wonders for buying stuff and you don't risk losing it all down the slippery slope of credit.

It is okay to be average. For God's sake, you can sit down and take a breath. You do not need to chase the idea of being the best, or being labeled high-achieving, or anything else. Do you know who makes Employee of the Month? People who make work their whole life. I'm not willing to do that anymore, and it's okay if you aren't either. Go home. Take a walk. Paint a picture. Have a dance party while you wash the dishes. You don't have to work late into the night to prove to your boss that you love her the most.

Stop competing and comparing. One of the best bosses I ever had kept a quote in her office from Theodore Roosevelt: "Comparison is the thief of joy." And it's true, whether you're comparing your life to somebody else's on social media, comparing your work output with a coworker's, or even comparing the way your boss gives praise between coworkers.

Stay in your lane, do your work, live your life. You don't have to achieve to the level of anyone around you, but you do have to do the level of work that makes you proud of yourself. No one else gets to decide what that is. You are developing the best you, and nobody else's opinion of you matters.

Chapter 7

Millennials Are Killing the Church

"Millennials leaving church in droves, study finds"

–CNN, May 2015

"Will Millennials Return to Religion?"

–*Publisher's Weekly*, **February 2018**

"Why we should worry when Millennials don't take religion seriously"

–*Washington Post*, **April 2015**

I wasn't raised in a religious household. My mother describes herself as "spiritual but not religious," my dad identifies as a "devout atheist," and I ping-ponged around, attending a day of Vacation Bible School with a friend down the street, going to church a couple times with friends or relatives, and becoming a practicing Wiccan in middle and high school before considering my religion a vague shrug and noncommittal surrender to the Universe. This chapter was co-written with a good friend and colleague of mine, Misty Watson, since I don't have a lot of first-hand experience interacting with the church myself.

Religion is so interesting to me, because I don't base any part of my identity on it. I believe in stuff, sure. The Universe, I usually call it. Not God, specifically, but not necessarily not-God, if that makes sense. I consider my spirituality an aspect of my life's practice but not my identity. And so, I see religion for what it truly is, and what it always has been, storytelling that gives people something to believe in.

I remember studying Greek and Roman mythology in high school and thinking that Christianity was no more or less valid than these stories. It's all mythology and belief systems, it's all just a way to find comfort in the unknown. Every civilization has their own idea of what happened before we got here, and people can find solace in those beliefs and the communities that surround them. No matter what your religious beliefs are, religion usually involves an aspect of community and togetherness that even atheists can appreciate. After all, humans are social creatures.

But what happens when those communities stop feeling so nurturing and supportive? What happens when your identity or your experience is shunned or ignored by the community, or even the God, you hold so dear?

Feeling Betrayed by God

According to the headlines, young people are leaving the church and turning their backs on organized religion. And data backs it up too: Research from PRRI comparing religious affiliation rates across decades show a massive rise in those claiming no affiliation. In 1986, only 10 percent of eighteen- to twenty-nine-year-olds were not religiously affiliated, while in 2016, 39 percent of this age range claimed no religion. That's four times as many Millennials opting out of organized religion as their counterparts thirty years ago.[35]

This is a phenomenon I've seen in action, first encountering it in a support group for Daughters of Narcissistic Mothers that also happened to focus on atheism and freethinking. Freethinking is a term that many atheists use to describe their rejection of religion, and I was struck by the Venn diagram of people who had experienced narcissistic abuse and people who rejected religion. It got me wondering why so many survivors of toxic parents were also atheists.

Then I realized that being raised as a child to respect an authority that will hand out whatever judgment it sees fit, regardless of how well you behave, is a pretty reasonable reason to reject the notion of God just as you've rejected the notion of loving parents. How can you rely on God when your own parents willfully hurt you, made you chase their approval, and turned a blind eye to your needs? I wouldn't be that into God either.

Here's where Misty comes in. Lacking the somewhat typical holier-than-thou-ism of your garden-variety Christian, I connected with her on a personal level of friendship and support and knew she'd speak to me candidly about her experiences with religion.

When asked about Millennials being less religious than past generations, Misty disagreed that this generation is any less religious. However, she thinks we're more open and honest about why we feel called to religion, and we have high expectations of our religious worship. She says, "My grandmother, who was born in 1934, will talk about how church connected her to her community and peers. But now we're so connected, we don't need church as our primary social outlet. We instead seek church or a group to help us grow and give us a sense of purpose."[36]

Of course. Millennials, once again, aren't content to just go sit in the same building their parents did and call it good enough. Millennials are socially engaged, highly altruistic, and believe in organizations and groups that have meaningful missions and values—whether that's church or a volunteer organization or a support group.

Of course Millennials aren't satisfied with church the way it has always been. We're not satisfied with anything the way it has always been.

Misty continued, "When we're confined to a building, we're not making a difference. So, we're less likely to attend church because church has become so confined to four walls. It's not about going out into the community and helping people, as it was when churches were founded after Christ's death."

If you belong to the Christian faith, it's just as easy to live your beliefs while serving or volunteering, helping those in need directly rather than plunking some change into the collection plate once a week. Non-churchgoing Christians can also reach out to online communities, read books and articles, and even incorporate mindfulness into their faith practice at home.

This brings up another consideration. Is mainstream Christianity a true reflection of what religion is really like? Christians have a stereotypical tendency to renounce those of different sexual orientation or gender identity, even those who belong to another religion or no religion. I remember a woman I volunteered with when I was in college, who told me, "Well, either you're right or I'm right, so I'll pray for your soul, just in case I'm right." Yikes.

Why should we worship and respect someone we can't see for the promise of future payoff?

Feeling Betrayed by the Church

Even if you still firmly believe in God's love and don't feel betrayed by God, it's easy to end up feeling betrayed by your church community. Misty shares her story of betrayal by the community that was supposed to be there for her.

The church has failed me horribly recently. I have been so let down by the church it has me questioning whether I still belong. My relationship with God is not shaken, but my relationship to the Seventh-day Adventist church is. I recently divorced. I don't feel comfortable saying why publicly because of my child, but my reasons shouldn't be questioned anyway. Instead of being comforted and supported through my darkest time, I was shunned. Some of my church members went so far as to block me on social media without ever asking me why I divorced or hearing my side of the story. I was stuck grieving not only the loss of my marriage, hopes, and dreams for my future, but the loss of my church family. These are the people I thought would support me the hardest and be there long after others left my side. Instead, they never arrived at my side at all.

Paul writes to us about the body of believers, the church. In 1 Corinthians 12:26, he says, "And if one member suffers, all the members suffer with it; or if one member is honored, all the members rejoice with it." I'm a part of the body. I never knew if I was considered an arm, a single vertebra, or the pinky toe, but the point is, I'm a part. But I suffered alone. "Rejoice with those who rejoice, and weep with those who weep," we're also told in Romans 12:15. Church members didn't run to my side to hold me up. None of them held me as I cried. None of them reassured that I would feel better soon, that I would get through this, that I had the strength I needed to not only survive but thrive again. I heard from two church members, once each. Both said they hated to see this happen, yet offered no other source of solace.

I had been a member there for twelve years. I taught the teens Sabbath School class for nearly eight of those years.

I helped with Vacation Bible School and other children's ministries. I did children's stories and Scripture reading for a time during the service. I quit only when my daughter became too clingy to handle me being up there where she could see me but not touch me. I was an integral part of the church. So I thought. The people who held me up and helped me trudge on weren't members of my church. They were pagans, spiritualists, and secular. Some believe in God. Some believe in Christ. But the people who held my hand, who let me cry on their shoulder, who sat in silence with me when I couldn't handle the isolation, weren't members of the Seventh-day Adventist Church.

–Misty Watson

Christianity Versus Christ

The thing about Christianity is that it's supposed to be a religion around the teachings of Christ. But a lot of people tend to use Christianity as a reason to judge people and lay on a thick layer of shame and hellfire when people do things they don't agree with. Isn't God supposed to do the judging? Don't Christians believe that Jesus died for our sins? I don't mean to mock religion, but it's hard not to mock its followers for being a big old pile of hypocrites who don't follow along with their favorite book.

These days it seems like Christianity is synonymous with the "Christian right," an identity rooted in political beliefs wrapped in hand-picked religion. Our society theoretically separates church and state (i.e., you can't legislate based on religion and there is no government-sanctioned official religion) and yet we still have arguments about abortion, birth control, and marriage based on religion, as if it's the deciding factor in how our country operates.

According to my friend, "Christ beautifully summed everything up for us simply in Matthew 22:37–40 when he said to love the Lord and love your neighbor as yourself. Everything else in Christianity hinges on those two ideas. If we're loving God first, then our neighbors (meaning everyone, literally every single person on this planet) as ourselves, then we're living for God. If we're truly doing those two things, everything else will fall into place. That was Christ's example to us."

And because Misty is amazing and totally gets the disconnect between her own faith and the so-called faith of the mainstream religious, she calls it right out. "How often do we talk to our peers and hear stories of those who have been harmed by the church? Instead of loving all, the church is shunning us. We can see it in politics, that people are using the word of God to harm other people. The word of God was never meant to harm others, but to bring us comfort and solace and give us guidance on how to live. So how can Millennials join a church if we're literally being hurt by being there? That's not part of God's plan."

This woman can seriously bring me around to the idea of organized religion when she starts laying the smackdown like this. One of my favorite Misty-isms is: "If your only reason for being a Christian is to tell people they're wrong, you're doing it wrong." She speaks specifically to those who hide behind Christianity when it comes to accepting (or not accepting) queer and gender-non-conforming individuals in the church. "No one can agree how to handle LGBTQ+ within the church. It is a hot-button issue that literally divides people. Bottom line? It doesn't matter what you think. It isn't up to you. Your only job on this earth when you profess your faith in Christ is to love him and to love your neighbor. Upon those two commandments hangs everything else. Until churches can see how legalistic and fundamentalist they are being, this issue won't be resolved."

When I was a resident assistant in college and the secretary for the Gay-Straight Alliance (long before I realized I wasn't straight), I was handing out pride pins and encouraging people to learn more about our organization. Two of my residents approached and I called them over, but once they realized what I was handing out, they quickly scurried away. I ended up having to have a mediation session between these two young women and myself with the assistant dean of students for housing in order to settle down their abject horror at the presence of gays, or something. I'm still not even sure what the problem was, but I do remember one of them wore a huge silver cross on a necklace, so I'm sure she thought I was going right to hell and taking her with me by proxy.

Considering the fact that interpretations of Christ's teachings vary from church to church, and it's always inclusion roulette when you walk through the doors and settle into a pew, I'm not really surprised so many Millennials have just stopped going. If you don't know you'll be accepted, why risk even trying? There are so many ways to explore religion and spirituality outside the church, while getting to help your greater community at the same time.

Representation in the Church

Misty is back again, this time with a first-hand account of the younger members of her congregation crying out for more diversity and representation to deaf ears.

> It feels like religion has fallen into the same trap as many other areas of our lives. We're screaming we need more representation, more POC, more young people, more women, and yet, the old white men are still calling the shots. Our church, the worldwide Seventh-day Adventist church, had a vote in recent years. They debated allowing women to be ordained as pastors. Now let me say, there were already women who had been ordained and were working as pastors. Some divisions said the church would have never grown as it did without women leading the way. And yet, at the end of it all, the vote came back "no" and it went so far as to say conferences who had ordained women would face harsh sanctions.
>
> No one was listening to us. During that entire debacle I'm not sure anyone in power actually heard the young or minority voices saying what they wanted—more diversity represented in the leadership of our church. I see the same thing in politics of course. When you see leadership, overwhelmingly, it is still older white men in those positions. There are exceptions. Things are changing. Slowly. But churches are not immune to that. And just like in other areas of our lives, we are saying this cannot continue and we refuse to be a part of a system that allows it to continue.
>
> Millennials are ready to hold offices. We're ready to take on leadership roles. We want to. Some of us are

approaching forty. We're not teenagers anymore. We're not even young, inexperienced adults anymore. But the older generation doesn't want to give up its position of power. This carries over into our churches.

—Misty Watson

Spirituality vs. Organized Religion

"Millennials haven't forgotten spirituality, they're just looking for new venues," says a PBS headline from a March 2017 interview.[37] The interview with Casper ter Kuile, a Harvard University researcher, discusses the fact that most Millennials aren't atheists, even if they have left the church. "Two-thirds believe in God or a universal spirit, and one in five even pray every day," says ter Kuile, speaking on Pew Research Center data regarding the one-third of Millennials who claim no religious affiliation.

This is something common among Millennials in my circles. It makes sense for humans to seek comfort in the unknown, and often that means a spiritual belief in God, the Universe, or any other way you want to talk about some cosmic force that offers spiritual guidance or something to snark at. I'm friends with Christians, witches, Jewish people, and probably a Muslim or two, with a handful of Buddhist-ish practitioners as well. I have always shied away from organized religion, often feeling awkward and unwelcome in a religious setting. I have always really enjoyed the spiritual aspect of faith, however.

I grew up with a bookshelf full of spirituality books. From astrology and tarot to Edgar Cayce to the complete collection of Wayne W. Dyer's philosophy and self-help books, my mother ran a one-woman library of spiritual education. She could spout off all sorts of things about living in the now and how "what you think about, you bring about." For better or worse, my mom was my gateway into spirituality and having a belief in some higher power without making it about God. She even took me to the local occult store for books on witchcraft and let me make an altar in my bedroom in my early teen years.

One aspect of universal spirituality is the Law of Attraction. There are countless books on the subject, including *The Secret,* which first brought this idea into the mainstream consciousness. The Law of Attraction is the idea that like attracts like. Meaning, if you're vibrating at a high frequency in life, grateful and positive and telling yourself how amazing your life is, you'll attract that lifestyle to yourself. Meanwhile, if you're vibrating at a low frequency, wracked with worry and shame over your less than stellar life, you'll continue to attract that low-vibe lifestyle in an inescapable vortex of shit shows.

While I appreciate the Law of Attraction from a gratitude and self-love standpoint, and I do believe that my positive attitude and knowledge that I will always get a great parking space is some low-level LOA in practice, I really can't get behind it when it comes to things going poorly. I have friends with disabilities, who are living as single parents after leaving abusive relationships, who have been assaulted multiple times, or who continue to be hired to new and exciting jobs only to realize that each one is somehow more demanding and crappy than the last. You can never convince me that these people are responsible for their own misfortunes because the Universe answered their negative woe-is-me call and heaped some more hardship on them like the cherry atop a struggle sundae.

I've tried just about every mindful and spiritual practice out there in the hopes of bringing myself a more positive and growth-oriented mindset. You can pick and choose what works for you and develop a spiritual practice that works for you.

How to Make Sure You're Killing It

Meditation is awesome. I know this because I keep reading about how awesome meditation is. I've tried a few guided meditations and really enjoyed them, but I also tend to kind of fall asleep or zone out completely, which might actually be the point? I plan to incorporate a regular meditation practice into my life and pick the habit back up, because it did make things feel calmer and more temporary whenever I found myself getting frustrated.

Affirmations work, if you believe them. I am a fan of positive affirmations. When I was trying to get pregnant with my second husband, I purchased an amethyst bracelet, and each time I noticed it throughout the day, I'd tell myself "My body knows how to conceive a healthy baby." It was a great way to remind myself to stay positive when all my brain wanted to do was spiral into chaos and gloom over the fact that my uterus couldn't work for some reason. As it turns out, my uterus just has great timing and I had no business getting pregnant with that guy. Sometimes the Universe will do you a solid. Practice affirmations related to what you want to receive more of in life. "I maintain a healthy weight effortlessly," "I am building a career that makes me feel happy to get up in the morning," "I give and receive love everywhere I go." Affirmations can help you achieve just a little bit more happiness and positivity in your day.

Gratitude journaling helps you focus on the little things. If you write down three things you're grateful for each morning and each night, you run out of big things fast. You start to think of the itty-bittiest things to be grateful for, like the feeling of warm grass underfoot in the summer, or the smell of a bonfire in the fall, or the fact that your cat has one really cute pink spotted paw pad and it's your favorite one of her paws. You could be grateful for your haunted refrigerator that makes a gurgly rattling noise at random intervals because it means you have fresh food. You could be grateful for a boss who doesn't mind if you're eight minutes late because you got stuck behind a school bus. The more you practice gratitude on a regular basis, the more you'll notice and appreciate the tiny things in life that make you smile.

Visualization is great for some people. I love imagining what my kick-ass life is going to look like when I manifest all the awesome things I deserve, but visualizing isn't a tactic that works for everyone. Some people just don't get anything from it. If you don't like the idea of visualizing mentally, try a vision board or sketchbook to make notes and collect images of the things you want from life. Make it your own.

Yoga is great for body and mind. Yoga is over five thousand years old and originated in India, but now Americans do it as part of their self-care routine and buy hundred-dollar yoga mats to prove how much they care about themselves. Snark aside, yoga is an amazing practice and something that can benefit nearly anyone. Look up some yoga videos online for free, or take a class at a gym or yoga studio near you. You don't have to do a super intense hot and sweaty yoga session to get the benefits of stretching and cycling through poses with mindful attention on your breath and body. Even if you can just do a few poses a day when you wake up and go to sleep, you'll notice you feel calmer and more relaxed during the day. That said, it's not going to replace your morning coffee. Drink up, buttercup.

Prayer can be helpful. No matter what you believe in, most spiritual and religious practices end up with some type of prayer. Whether it's simply surrendering to the Universe, lighting a candle and praying to a deity of your choice, or kneeling before bedtime to speak with Christ, there's evidence that prayer helps people feel more positive. The surrender of your worldly problems to a higher power gives you the ability to put down your worries about what you can't control.

Church isn't what makes you religious. If you want to go to church, go to church. If you don't, don't. Your participation in a church setting has nothing to do with your religious faith. You're in the driver's seat here, so make your faith what you want it to be in a way that's meaningful to you.

Respect others. This is a major tenet of every religion. Harm none. Judge not. Treat others as you wish to be treated. If someone is different from you, don't assume they're driving the bus to hell with all the other sinners. Maybe open up and learn something instead.

The extremists do not define the religion. Westboro Baptists don't represent every Baptist, just like extremists who harm others don't represent everyone from their religion. Bad people are bad people, no matter what religion they claim. Don't fall for media tropes about how some religions are out to get us. Yes, I'm talking about Muslims.

Experience other cultures. Go on a tour of a local mosque or synagogue to immerse yourself in the unknown. Maybe you won't be so scared. Pro tip: You may be asked to cover your head or remove your shoes, so don't be surprised. Grab some pamphlets, do some reading, and learn something new!

Part III

Millennials Are Just Making Stuff Up Now

Chapter 8

Millennials Are Killing Gender

"Are Millennials Gender Rebels or Returning to Tradition?"

–Phys.org, January 2018

"Are Millennials Putting an End to Gender Differences?"

–*Newsweek*, **November 2017**

"Gender loses its impact with the young"

–*USA Today*, **June 2014**

T he number one rule of the internet is "Don't read the comments section," but I still find myself pulled into that train wreck time and time again. Unfortunately, comments on already painful articles about bullying and suicide and murder become even more heinous when the victim is transgender or nonconforming to the gender they were assigned at birth. Millennials are hardly the first generation to experience and acknowledge transgender identities, but like most things, we do things loudly in our special snowflake way and tend to ruffle the feathers of those who came before us and insist that "guys" is gender-neutral and that everyday people just trying to pee and live their lives are lurking in women's restrooms to molest children.

Here are some statements that I personally have witnessed, either in person or said via social media to people I know, regarding gender:

- I just don't get why "they" go by "they" when "they" look so feminine.

- I can't wrap my head around "they" as a pronoun, it's grammatically incorrect.

- There's no way a child can know they are transgender, that's the parents forcing their ideas on the kid.

- "Guys" is gender-neutral.

- I'll stop saying "guys" or "dude" if someone tells me it hurts them, but until then I see no reason to stop using it as a gender-neutral term.

- I consider myself a transhumanist, which means that I believe that our society will advance to the point that sexism and racism and gender aren't a problem anymore, so I don't see a reason to be worried about it now.

How hard is it to just call people by the names and pronouns they use for themselves? It's so simple and it doesn't affect your life at all, aside from a moment of embarrassment if you make a mistake. But it's easier, and far more compassionate, to correct yourself instead of making this your hill to die on and telling the person you've misgendered or misnamed that you're a good person and it's their fault for not being telepathic and letting you know before they spoke.

As a cisgender white woman who passes as straight 90 percent of the time, my opinions on this matter are not the definitive authority on gender issues. However, as a cisgender white woman who passes as straight, it's kind of on me to round up all the people in my circle and use the fact that you're reading my book to tell you to do better for your queer and trans friends. Even the best ally still has work to do.

Boys Will Be Boys

I want to slam my head against a wall when I hear this phrase and its adult counterpart, "locker-room talk." These excuses let men and boys off the hook for inappropriate behavior, from bullying to sexual assault, throughout their lifetimes. From Brock Turner to Donald Trump, boys being boys means that it's okay to assault a woman because, like, what else do you expect a dude to do?

We let our boys down when we raise them to act without thinking, do what they want without consequence, and act out with violence instead of expressing emotions. We raise little girls to be demure and polite and quiet, while boys get to tumble and climb and build and roar. This is some gendered bullshit.

I tried to conceive a baby with my second husband for over eighteen months. When I moved out in advance of our divorce, I brought all the baby stuff I had accumulated with me. I didn't know what to do with it. I ended up giving away hundreds of dollars' worth of baby supplies, save for a handful of items: a woven wrap I spent way too much money on, and two items of clothing. One is a teal onesie that says, "tiny feminist," and the other is a black tee shirt that says, "boys will be held accountable just like girls." Regardless of sex or gender, my kids will be raised as inclusive feminists. We need more people raising their kids as inclusive feminists.

Inclusive Feminism

I want to include a brief note on feminism. Some people out there exclude trans women from their feminist spaces, spouting off some nonsense about how trans women have male privilege and aren't truly women. This idea can go walk off a bridge. Feminism is for all women and for all people. Feminism helps men too, by rejecting the idea that boys and men who are in tune with their emotional needs are "girly" and therefore weak.

Emotions are emotions: anger, sadness, happiness, fear, anxiety... these are all normal things for any person to feel. Stop gendering feelings, just feel them.

Gendered from Birth

I have a confession: I think gender reveal parties are weird. Finding out the sex of your baby at the doctor's office is one thing, but throwing a whole party centered around gendered themes strikes me as odd. Of course, do what you want to do, because it's not my baby and it's not my life, but these parties lead down a rabbit hole of aggressively gendered stereotypes. Here are some of my favorites, found with a quick Google search:

- Touchdowns or Tutus
- Guns or Glitter
- Pistols or Pearls
- Cupcake or Stud Muffin
- Bows or Arrows
- Wheels or Heels
- Boots or Bows
- 'Staches or Lashes
- Quarterback or Cheerleader

What I have learned in this brief foray into baby gender is that girl babies must wear frilly and sparkly tulle outfits, be dipped in sugar, wear bows and mascara, cheer, wear high heels but *not* boots, and are somehow an arrow. Or are they the bow? I am not sure how that one works. Meanwhile, boy babies can shoot things, ride things, wear weather-appropriate footwear, play sports, and grow a mustache. We already start to place stereotypes and gender roles on children before they are born. Little girls get pink and soft things and dolls, little boys get blue and dinosaurs and messages about being tough and messy. Have you ever seen children play? They all jump in the mud, climb trees, and run around until they fall over tired. They throw things and play tag and play house and play kitchen. Gender has nothing to do with it, yet we insist on starting as soon as possible with making sure the colors and toy options are right, because God forbid the kid have any preferences of their own.

Millennial parents are leaning into allowing their children the autonomy to express themselves however they like, as long as nobody's getting hurt. Boys with long hair? Sure! Girls who want to play sports? Absolutely. Boys playing with dolls, taking ballet classes, and dressing up as a princess for Halloween? Yes, please. Girls who like to play wrestle and climb the highest tower on the playground? Indeed. Hair, activities, toys, and clothes are not inherently gendered. If you're a boy wearing a dress, that's a boy's dress. If you're a girl who wants to be an astronaut when she grows up, that's a woman's career. We hold our children back when we place limits on their expression and dreams based solely on what's in their pants.

Gender vs. Sex

Speaking of what's in their pants, it ain't gender.

I once had a cat who had urinary tract issues. He had a recurring blockage, which is fatal if left untreated. I ended up draining my vacation savings to pay for emergency surgery, which I was told would widen the opening of his urethra. In a more detailed consultation with the vet, I realized this widening happened because they removed the entire penis in order to remove the portion of his urethra that was narrower and prone to blockage.

My esteemed husband at the time described this process as "turning our boy cat into a girl cat," to my immediate and never-ending eye rolls. Then, when I described the surgery to a friend of mine, she told me that she knew a human, non-cat, man who'd had a similar surgery after urinary tract issues. Egad, but this man still identified with his gender even after losing his penis? Yes, because gender isn't in your genitals. Gender is in your brain.

Before I dive into more detailed goodies about gender theory, I want to provide a glossary of terms you can refer to if this expanding vocabulary isn't something you've heard before. Stick with me.

AFAB or **AMAB**: Assigned female at birth or assigned male at birth. These terms have replaced what used to be known as FTM or MTF (female to male or male to female). Using "assigned at birth" correctly identifies that the "change" in gender was in fact a mistake at birth. A trans woman has always been a woman, even if she was assigned male pronouns and a male identity at birth. The assignment was incorrect.

Agender: Not identifying as a man or woman, an agender identity may fall under the nonbinary or genderqueer labels. This term is a true neutral of gender identity.

Cisgender: Identifying with the gender assigned to you at birth.

Deadname: The legal and/or birth name of a person who now goes by a different name. Don't deadname somebody. If you knew them before and after transition, refer to them as their chosen name regardless of if you knew them by a different name before.

Genderfluid: Someone who is genderfluid fluctuates between different gender identities and expressions. They may strongly identify with aspects of two or more genders.

Gender Nonconforming: Someone whose gender identity does not conform with their gender assignment at birth or societal expectations of their gender. Also called gender variance.

Genderqueer: Basically, any or all of the above. Someone who is genderqueer may identify as two or more genders simultaneously, may switch or fluctuate between genders, may have no gender at all, or may otherwise identify as gender nonconforming.

Nonbinary: Abbreviated as "NB" or "enby," nonbinary means that a person does not identify as a man or woman, but rather outside the gender binary of choosing either male or female-ness.

Singular They: The use of the third person plural pronoun "they" as a singular pronoun to replace "he" or "she" when addressing or speaking about a person who is nonbinary or gender nonconforming. Not all nonconforming people like "they," so be sure to ask for pronouns if you don't know!

Transgender: Identifying with a gender other than the one assigned to you at birth.

-X: Ending a word with an x is a gender-neutral signifier. It can be used in place of Mr./Ms. (using the term Mx. instead), Latino/a (using the term Latinx instead), or is increasingly used as an alternative to "folks" (using folx instead) to signify inclusion of any and all genders in a group.

Everything you thought you knew about gender is wrong. This is why people think Millennials are just making up a bunch of new words to trap people into a checkmate of political correctness. Really, it's just words to explain things that have been happening for years and years, and it's finally safe to start talking about these topics out loud.

Gender identity is based on how you in particular define your gender as a man, woman, neither, or both. These definitions are obviously limited by the aspects of what society considers being a man or being a woman, and they're really up to you as an individual. Your gender identity has nothing to do with your genitals, but for the record: someone with a vagina, uterus, ovaries, etc. is typically assigned female at birth, and someone with a penis, testes, etc. is typically assigned male at birth. For a lot of people, these assignments make sense to them and they identify with the gender they were assigned at birth. Cool! For a lot of other people, these assignments don't match the way they feel about themselves and they identify with another gender. Cool!

Gender is assigned at birth based on biological sex, and sex is characterized by things like hormones, chromosomes, and body factors like voice, muscle and fat patterns, bone density, body hair, etc. But sex and gender don't always match. I know men who have given birth and women with penises, I know people who wear dresses and lack gender, I know people who started their transition in their fifties and are finally living an authentic life that's true to their identity. I know parents who allow their children to go by different names and wear the clothes they want because they feel more like a girl or don't feel like either. The freedom to express how you feel inside is beautiful and should be celebrated.

Unfortunately, in our modern society, there's an undercurrent of transphobic panic.

The Risks of Gender Nonconformity

When faced with someone who is different from what you've experienced and what you've been raised to believe, you have a couple options. The first option is to be curious, open-minded, and accepting of someone's differences. The second is to be afraid, closed-minded, and reject them because they don't jibe with your expectations of what people are like.

Imagine you were raised in a small town and then went to the big city for college. You're going to meet a lot of new people and be faced with a lot of new ideas. Wouldn't it be silly to just assume all of those people are somehow broken because they're not what you expected them to be like? Just because they're not like you? We grow when we face new information about the world and learn more about it. We stagnate when we choose to live in a deliberately exclusive echo chamber.

Being transgender in today's world is not very safe, even in the United States. Men have murdered trans women on dates, trans youth commit suicide and experience bullying at outrageous rates, and the overall life expectancy of a trans person is lower than their cisgender counterparts—especially trans people of color, who experience an even more disproportionate risk of violence.

According to the 2015 US Transgender Survey, a survey of nearly twenty-eight thousand people, transgender or gender nonconforming individuals reported the following forms of discrimination, violence, and mistreatment.[38]

- 10 percent reported that a family member was violent toward them
- 8 percent were kicked out of their family homes due to their gender identity
- If they were out during their K-12 school years, 54 percent were verbally harassed, 24 percent were physically attacked, and 13 percent were sexually assaulted because they were transgender
- 17 percent left school due to their mistreatment
- 30 percent of employed respondents reported being fired, denied a promotion, or experiencing other forms of discrimination including harassment and physical or sexual assault at work
- 47 percent of respondents were sexually assaulted in their lifetime, and 10 percent reported a sexual assault in the last year
- 29 percent of transgender respondents live in poverty (compared to 12 percent of the overall United States population) and 15 percent are unemployed (compared to 5 percent of the overall United States population)
- Compared to 63 percent of the US population, only 16 percent of trans respondents own a home

- 30 percent of trans individuals have experienced homelessness in their lifetime, and 12 percent have experienced homelessness in the last year

- 39 percent experienced serious psychological distress in the month prior to the survey, compared to 5 percent of the overall US population

- 40 percent have attempted suicide in their lifetime, compared to 4.6 percent of the overall US population

- 33 percent have had a negative experience with a healthcare provider including being harassed or refused treatment, and 23 percent did not seek needed healthcare in the last year due to fear of harassment or discrimination

Diving even deeper, the survey confirmed that transgender people of color and transgender people with disabilities experience even starker odds.

- 43 percent of Latinx respondents, 41 percent of American Indian respondents, 40 percent of multiracial respondents, and 38 percent of Black respondents live in poverty

- 20 percent of transgender people of color are unemployed

- 6.7 percent of Black respondents, and 19 percent of Black trans women live with HIV, compared to 1.4 percent of all survey respondents and 0.3 percent of the overall US population

- 24 percent of undocumented respondents were physically assaulted in the year prior to the survey

- 50 percent of undocumented respondents have experienced homelessness in their lifetime

- 68 percent of undocumented respondents have experienced domestic violence

- 24 percent of respondents with disabilities are unemployed and 45 percent live in poverty

- Over half (59 percent) of transgender people with disabilities report current serious psychological distress and 54 percent have attempted suicide in their lifetime

- 42 percent of transgender people with disabilities report mistreatment by healthcare providers

It's worth mentioning that the survey respondents are people who are still living their lives. Transgender people and transgender people of color are disproportionately the victims of homicides and hate crimes in the US.

According to a 2016 survey by the National Coalition of Anti-Violence Programs (NCAVP), "Continuing an alarming multiyear trend, people of color, transgender and gender nonconforming people made up the majority of victims of LGBTQ and HIV-affected related hate violence." Including the forty-nine victims of the Pulse shooting in Orlando, NCAVP investigated the details of seventy-seven hate violence homicides in 2016. Of the twenty-eight non-Pulse hate crimes, 79 percent were people of color, 68 percent were transgender or gender nonconforming, and 61 percent were transgender women of color. A staggering 61 percent of victims were under age thirty-five (i.e., Millennials or younger).[39]

I'm at a loss to turn these statistics into some positive message beyond a plea to please stop being assholes to people who are different than you. No one should die or be turned away from medical care or be made homeless because of their identity. What is wrong with us that we think this is okay?

The only way to combat the societal acceptance of discrimination and hate crimes is to normalize nonconforming identities.

As long as trans people are seen as less-than, mentally ill, or otherwise weird, different, or threatening to the status quo, people will continue to treat them as such. Again, I say, please stop being assholes.

Transgender Representation in the Media

Part of the reason Millennials are so noisy and seemingly obnoxious about changing the political landscape and making space for people who are different is because we have the glorious and all-connecting internet. For every troll living under an internet bridge, there is an equal or larger number of supportive and safe people who are doing their best to change the landscape.

And it is our job as supportive and safe people to change the landscape. Trans people are doing enough work just living their lives. We have to show up, spread the word, call out transphobic jokes and comments when we encounter them, and share inclusive media in our social circles.

There's no lack of amazing and inclusive webcomics, video content, and Tumblr posts to go around, but gender inclusion has also hit the mainstream in exciting ways that make all the broflakes really grumpy. Marvel has passed Thor's hammer to a female hero, and the new lead of BBC's *Doctor Who* is finally a female Doctor. And yet, many people young and old find reasons to whine about the gender of fictional alien characters. If they can't get over it in fiction, we have a long way to go for people to get over it in real life.

We're even gender inclusive in our cartoons now, too! *Steven Universe* features a cast of characters who are essentially sentient, sexless gemstones from outer space, though they do use she/her pronouns. The show, aired on Cartoon Network, is widely celebrated for its depictions of non-heteronormative relationships, rejection of traditional gender roles, and inclusion of gender nonconforming characters. This cartoon is beloved by children and adults alike, many of whom wish media like this existed when they were but wee kids trying to understand why they felt so damn different.

If you can't get the adults to wrap their heads around inclusion, compassion, and empathy, it's a good idea to start with the kids. Kids inherently understand that differences are okay and aren't something that affect how to interact with the world. You can tell a little kid anything and they just get it. When you're a kid, everything is normal. We could learn so much from the children if we just opened up our minds.

How to Make Sure You're Killing It

Use inclusive language. When addressing a group, instead of "guys" or "ladies," try "friends," "team," or another non-gendered term. Default to gender-neutral terms in your daily life, rather than waiting for someone to ask you to do this. It goes a long way toward being a safe person and a true ally.

Apologize when you make a mistake. If you misgender someone or accidentally call them by their deadname, simply apologize and correct yourself. Making it a huge deal will call more attention to the situation and likely make your friend feel awkward and uncomfortable. Don't make your embarrassment their problem, just make it right as quickly as possible and move along.

Ask for people's pronouns. When you're first meeting someone, it's okay to ask for pronouns or provide your own. Since anyone could identify as any gender, making it a norm to introduce yourself with pronouns means that people will feel safe to trust you with their own.

Be safe to come out to. If someone comes out to you as transgender or gender nonconforming, be calm and awesome about it. Try: "That's great! How can I help you feel supported during your transition?" "That's awesome, I'm so proud of you!" Avoid grilling them about how long they've been sitting on this news or if they're going to get surgery or start hormone therapy. They will keep you in as much of the loop as they want. Don't be nosy, just be supportive.

Think outside the binary. Catch yourself before you call tampons "lady supplies" or refer to something as only affecting men or women.

Don't overthink the past. If you knew someone before their transition, you might be tempted to say, "Back when he was a woman," or "When Jack was Jackie," or something like this. Don't. Your friend was always your friend as they are now, even if they went by a different name or were trying to conform to another gender. They trusted you with their identity as it developed and as they became their authentic self, so don't drag that trust through the mud by deadnaming them in the name of an accurate timeline. Just say, "Before she/he/they transitioned."

Support your trans friends. You probably know a trans person living in poverty or who has health issues that keep them from doing much. Pay attention to their needs and do what you can to help support them, so they don't feel so alone. Whether it's a pizza, something off their Amazon wish list, their electric bill, ordering something from their home-based business, or just sending them a really nice note, do something kind for your trans friends today.

Support your trans friends even when they aren't looking. If you're with someone who makes a transphobic comment or joke, uses gender as an insult or way to demean something, or is otherwise being exclusive and shitty, call them out.

Do not release balloons. You can have a gender reveal party if you want, but balloons are terrible for the environment. Don't do it.

Chapter 9

Millennials Are Killing Flirting

"Is #MeToo the End of Flirting as We Know it?"

—The Good Men Project, June 2018

Yes all women." It's a rallying cry. It's support. It's a demand to be seen and heard. Every woman has experienced sexual harassment in her lifetime. School dress codes penalize girls for showing too much shoulder or knee, insisting they'll distract the boys (or worse, the male teachers). We lack basic education around consent from childhood, forcing hugs on kids or insisting that "he's just picking on you because he likes you." When strange men shout at women on the street, they insist it's a compliment and she must be a bitch for being rude about it. Hey, sweetheart, smile!

With the explosion of the #MeToo movement, originally created by Tarana Burke in 2007 and popularized by actor Alyssa Milano in 2017, it appeared that people finally felt secure and supported enough to reveal some of their darkest secrets about surviving sexual assault. From Harvey Weinstein, Louis C.K., and Kevin Spacey all the way to Brett Kavanaugh and Donald Trump, big names were under fire and being publicly held accountable for their actions in a way we've never seen before. While Millennials cannot and do not take credit for the #MeToo movement, we have participated and boosted the signal. Because we have all either been harassed or know someone who has been harassed.

Of course, cis women aren't the only victims of harassment, as mentioned in the chapter on gender. Trans and nonconforming individuals experience a much higher risk of harassment and assault than cis women, and transmisogyny runs rampant in our society. Boo, cis dudes.

A close and very dear friend of mine shared a story of surviving a rape, and I left a comment telling her I believed her and I'm here for her. I see these stories constantly. I know countless people who are survivors of multiple rapes and assaults, and it's harrowing and heartbreaking to see how common sexual assault is in 2018. After I commented, she sent me a message including an image her grandmother had shared online that morning: "As long as women who accuse men of sexual attacks are believed without evidence or due process, no man is safe. I'm not safe. Your husband isn't safe. Your father isn't safe. Your son isn't safe. Your grandson isn't safe. Your male friends aren't safe. #HimToo."

While, yes, men do experience sexual harassment too, derailing important conversations about rape culture and harassment of non-cis men is completely missing the point. According to Stop Street Harassment, 77 percent of women have experienced verbal sexual harassment (34 percent of men), 51 percent of women have been touched or groped (17 percent of men), and 27 percent of women have survived sexual assault (7 percent of men).[40]

Harassment and assault also disproportionately affect gay, lesbian, and bisexual people compared to their heterosexual counterparts. The CDC's National Intimate Partner and Sexual Violence Survey reported that 44 percent of lesbians and 61 percent of bi women experience rape, physical violence, or stalking compared to 35 percent of straight women. Also, 46 percent of bisexual women have survived rape compared to 17 percent of straight women and 13 percent of lesbian women. Additionally, 22 percent of bisexual women report rape by an intimate partner, compared to 9 percent of straight women. The trend of harassment against bisexual people carries over into the male statistics as well: 26 percent of gay men and 37 percent of bisexual men experience rape, physical violence, or stalking (29 percent straight), and 40 percent of gay men and 47 percent of bisexual men have experienced sexual violence other than rape (21 percent straight).[41]

I covered rates of harassment and mistreatment of transgender individuals in the last chapter, and sexual harassment also disproportionately affects them. The 2015 US Transgender Survey reported that 47 percent of transgender people are sexually assaulted during their lifetime—that's basically half. If you know two trans people, one of them has been assaulted. Check on your trans friends, please.

This #HimToo song and dance is patently ridiculous on several levels, but it was almost exactly what I was thinking about when I sat down to write this chapter. Men feel unsafe because women are reporting and calling out sexual assaults and harassments. They feel unsafe to ask a woman out, make a move, or even flirt. Because, like, what if she screams rape when he asks for her number?

Please.

I will go into a lot more detail around dating in the next chapter, but I wanted to specifically address the idea that men feel "unsafe" flirting with women now. I've heard men say things like, "You can't flirt with women or tell them you're interested, because they'll think you're a creep who is harassing them." Even *Superman* actor Henry Cavill kept digging himself a hole on this topic, saying, "Well, I don't want to go up and talk to her, because I'm going to be called a rapist or something."

Let me be totally clear, Henry and all other men: if you're afraid somebody is going to call you a rapist for flirting with them, you are doing it wrong. Maybe do a little introspection and make sure you're not being a total fucking creep.

Catcalling Is Not Flirting

I usually run on nature trails in my area, in the early morning with a friend. Before this dedication to the buddy system and running before the world wakes up was as firmly planted, sometimes I'd run by myself through my neighborhood. With the sun up. This happened exactly one time before some dude leaned out of his red pickup truck at a stop sign and said, "Hey sweetie!" before revving his engine and speeding away. Even though he never approached me and never said anything about my body, I felt extremely unsettled. I was out running, listening to music, clearly busy doing something. And this guy just felt the need to roll down his window and shout at me.

Catcalling is not flirting. It's not a compliment. It's not sexy. Never in the history of ever has a woman swooned over being shouted at from a car or across the road about how nice her ass looks in her jeans. She knows how good her ass looks in her jeans, that's why she likes those jeans. Those jeans are not for you to scream at.

I asked my friends on Facebook if they've ever been catcalled and to share their stories if they were willing. Within ten minutes I had as many stories. One story was less than two hours old and had happened just that morning.

My friend was parked in her car with the window down and a man said, "Goddamn, I've seen sexy, but you? You fucking sexy as fuck. Goddamn." She turned her head away from him and he continued, "Don't you turn your head at me while I try to give you a compliment. Goddamn, you sexy as fuck, woman." She pulled her car out of the space, and he still kept going, "Hey, come back here. I wanna talk to you." She kept driving away. When she shared her story, she also added that this interaction did not make her feel attractive, nor did she like the attention. It made her feel like she was about to be assaulted.

Another friend was walking near her house while wearing her baby in a carrier when a car pulled up behind her, screeched to a stop, and started honking. The driver whistled and yelled out the window. My friend turned around and the car sped off, but the driver came back a second time, singing a song and yelling to her over the music. The driver didn't leave her alone until she reached the main road, and she cut her walk short and kept her phone in hand the entire way home in case she needed to dial 911.

Yet another friend was walking in the early morning with headphones in. She wasn't playing any music, but the headphones usually acted as a deterrent to anyone bothering her. Unfortunately, she heard a man whistle loudly at her and she turned her head when she heard the sound but kept walking. The man caught up to her and pulled her headphones out. She smiled at him, he called her a stuck-up slut, she *apologized to him*, and he shook his head and walked away.

Tired of stories yet? Too bad. Here's another one. She was walking at night with a friend and a man drove by in a truck and yelled

"Hey sexy," to which she responded "FUCK OFF" in a blind rage. She says she shouldn't have given him the extra attention, even if it felt good in the moment to finally fight back. *Finally,* as in, this has happened before, and she has always just taken it in stride and kept walking.

Catcalling is not about flirting or complimenting women, it's about men reminding women that we are here for their consumption and appreciation. Like we are pieces in an art museum they can muse at. But I've never seen any man shout, "Goddamn, I've seen art, but this is some fucking art!" at a van Gogh.

Van Gogh fuck yourself, creepy dudes. (Yes, I know it's pronounced "Goff," but I don't care.)

Power Plays Are Not Flirting

Men preying on younger women or girls, or cornering women to get them alone, is also not about flirting. It's about finding an easy target, which is gross and creepy. Any physical intimidation, including cornering, touching without consent, or blocking women so they can't easily get away, is harassment. And using age (or "maturity"), income, or grand sweeping gestures to convince a woman you're a worthy partner is at best a little much, and at worst, coercive.

Our dad used to take us to a local bar on his custody weekends, and since I aged out of those, my sister got four extra years of bar dates with Dad. Once when she was about fifteen, she was doodling on a sheet of paper at a bar when a man came up and complimented her artwork. He sat next to her and told her about how much money he had, and our dad's friend Freddy was sitting on the other side of her on a stool, keeping an eye on the interaction. Dad came over and chatted with the man, whom he appeared to be familiar with, and introduced her as his daughter, indicating her young age. Dad left again, and the man resumed his creepy flirtations. Freddy told the dude to back off and the guy refused, so Freddy ended up making his suggestion a little more physical when he punched the guy, who promptly left the bar, never to be seen again.

Another friend shared a story from when she was a young teenager, maybe fourteen or fifteen years old. A neighbor in his twenties would follow her around the apartment complex, and once cornered her by the pool to kiss her cheek and tell her she was pretty. He tried to get her to go into the bathroom with him, but her dog growled at the man and she was able to get away.

Yet another woman in my circle shared her story. A man sat next to her at a bar, put his hand on her leg, looked at her and asked, "You're on birth control, right?" Dude, you cannot just touch people and ask invasive questions.

Early-morning harassment seems to be a theme among these men who just want to pay women a nice compliment and ask them out. One friend used to catch an early bus to get to work by six, and one day the bus was early and empty. The driver passed by the next stop without stopping, then missed a turn at a major intersection on the route. My friend pulled the cord to ring for a stop and the driver ignored her until he pulled onto a tiny side road ten miles outside the city near deserted farms. He turned to look at her and said, "Alone at last! I've been trying to ask you out for weeks. Shall we go get breakfast?" As he stood up and turned to walk back to her seat, she was out of the back door of the bus in seconds. The driver yelled, "Oh come on, let's go out! How else are you getting back to town?" She ran and flagged down a truck for a ride to a gas station to call the police and the bus company. The police found the bus, but not the driver, and the driver had put in notice to quit at the end of the day, so the bus company wouldn't do anything.

One of my best friends also shared a story of when she used to wait tables at a family restaurant. A regular, old enough to be her grandpa, would compliment her and ask when she was going to marry him. He asked if she had a boyfriend and told her boys her age didn't appreciate her and that when she was older she'd have her pick.

These are not cute anecdotes of harmless flirtation. These stories are men forcing themselves onto women, leaving lifelong impressions and trauma on the survivors. If you ask your circle for stories of sexual harassment and assault, you will be shocked (or not) at the sheer volume of stories you receive. Remember: We're not afraid to make noise when we are mistreated. Calling it out is safer than ever before.

Believe and support survivors.

How to Make Sure You're Killing It

I am the last person to ask about flirting advice, because I'm pretty sure I am terrible at it. But since we seem to need a how-to manual on modern-day flirting and giving compliments, I'll do my best.

Compliment something the person has control over. Compliment someone's skills, style, wardrobe, or hair. Do so without making it about you or about their body/attractiveness and *do so without expecting anything in return.* "Your haircut is awesome!" "Those boots are rad!" and "That top is amazing!" are positive compliments, while "Short hair is so sexy," "Those boots make your legs look great," and "That top really works for you" are, uh, less so. A note on body positivity: You'd be surprised how shitty "You can really pull off that top," and "That's a super flattering skirt" can feel to people who have larger bodies that the world hates. Stick to, once again, complimenting their overall style or look without making it a commentary on how brave they are for wearing stripes or large patterns in the light of day.

Pay attention to social cues. If you give someone a compliment and they respond, "Thank you!" then they are done with the conversation and it is time to go. They do not owe you their time or energy. If they want to have a conversation about it, that's up to them. "Awesome tattoo!" can lead to "Thanks!" or it might lead to "Thanks! My best friend has a shop in town, and I go there for all my work," which can open the door to a conversation if you're both into it. Maybe you'll make a friend. Maybe you can ask for a number.

Smiling is not consent. I love to run outside. Frequently, when two people pass each other on a trail, they'll typically nod or smile, maybe wave, maybe say good morning. But I don't say "Hey, how's your day going?" or "You look great in those shorts, can I get your number?" If you wouldn't disturb someone while they're running or working out, don't disturb them when they are otherwise occupied with living their life. This includes sitting on a bus or subway, walking down the street, grocery shopping, reading a book on a bench, working at their job, or literally existing.

Stop telling women to smile. It's fucking weird, and men don't tell each other to smile the way they tell women to smile. I was in a shop once, and a guy looked at me and said, "Oh, how was the funeral?" When I looked at him with a "WTF" look on my face, he said something about how I should smile, and I left the store.

Headphones mean "do not disturb." If someone has their headphones on, don't bother them, unless there is a large bee or a fire or a chainsaw murderer they need to be aware of. They are doing their own thing, many of them are coping with social anxiety or reducing the sensory overload of being near large groups of people. Invading their space will make them feel uncomfortable nine times out of ten.

No unsolicited naughty pics. If someone wants to see your penis, they will ask nicely.

If you are ignored, move along. If you give a compliment to someone, or say hello, or smile, and they ignore you, just go on about your day. If your instinct is to shout, "Say hello, you stuck-up bitch," you are not a nice person. That's not flirting, that's demanding attention, and it makes you a creep. See item number one—don't expect anything in return.

It's okay to state your interest. If you're feeling a spark and want to ask someone out on a date, do so. Be straightforward and just ask. "I'd love to schedule a coffee date with you sometime, would you like that?" But, keep in mind…

It's okay for them to say no. If you ask someone out, they have every right in the world to say no. Maybe they are too stressed or busy. Maybe they aren't romantically available or looking for dates right now. Maybe they just don't want to go on a date with you. All of these things are about them and their decisions, which, fun fact, they are in charge of. If you feel rejected, that's okay. "I'm disappointed but I completely understand. Thank you for letting me know you're not interested" goes a lot better than tirades about how you're such a nice guy and they owe you a date because you're just so nice.

IT IS OKAY FOR THEM TO SAY NO. At any time, during any activity. If they say yes to a date in the first place, then change their mind, that's okay. If they say yes to a date, then go on the date, and they say no to a second date, that's okay. If they say yes to a date, go home with you, and decide they're not into the makeout sesh, that's okay. Learn the word "no." It means "no."

Get consent. For top-notch flirting, make sure the person consents to the conversation. Sidle up next to them at the bar and say, "Hey, do you mind if I chat with you while I wait for my food?" instead of saying, "Hey baby, come here often?" If you ask right away if they're in the space for a conversation, that shows from minute one that you believe in their autonomy and consent. Don't force anything on someone, even a conversation. It's not hard to ask!

Take no for an answer the first time. Wearing somebody down into saying yes for a drink with you is not consent, and it's not nice to do. My sister was repeatedly asked out by a coworker who wouldn't take no for an answer, and she finally agreed to get a drink with him. He sexually assaulted her at the bar, forcing her against a wall and kissing her after she said she didn't want to kiss him. "No" is a complete sentence. Learn it.

Chapter 10

Millennials Are Killing Relationships

"How Millennials Have Killed Modern Romance"

—Thought Catalog, February 2017

"Are Millennials Ruining Dating?"

—The Odyssey Online, February 2016

'm a thirty-year-old divorcee. Not only that, I am a thirty-year-old divorcee times two. Yes, I have "gotten it wrong" two times, once at twenty-one and once at twenty-eight, and somehow, I'm still undecided on the idea of marriage in the future. Maybe it's that childhood song that goes, "First comes love, then comes marriage, then comes baby in the baby carriage" that helps me continue to wax poetic over the idea of promising to legally bind myself to another human for the rest of my life, probably, if I don't decide to legally unbind. But at this point, I could just as easily go the other way.

Plus, it's 2018. We all know it doesn't always go love, marriage, baby carriage. These days, love might not lead to marriage or even long-term commitment, and some of us aren't having babies at all. Since the advent of internet dating, romance starts on a screen, with a casual meeting that might progress into a relationship, a friendship with benefits, or maybe the proverbial marriage and a baby carriage. But there is no set trajectory for courtship. In fact, the development of my relationship with my boyfriend seems to have sprung from the mind of a romcom writer's pitch room.

Fade in. We see a man open his dating app and type in "vegan" to search for local veggie chicks. He unironically eats kale. We see a woman browsing through dating app profiles. She checks her messages and sees that a reasonably attractive dude has asked her about her favorite vegan taco options. They begin a conversation. They meet up and hit all four Millennial bases in one date: (1) sex, (2) being seen together in daylight, (3) sharing childhood trauma, and (4) expressing romantic interest. Plus, he made a vegan tiramisu.

Within four months, they're talking cohabitation. Occasionally one will ask, "Is this crazy?" and they'll conclude that everything actually feels really solid and comfortable. Then they have to start a *Jay and Silent Bob*-type mission to go find everyone who said, "You'll find it when you stop looking for it!" because it is really, really annoying that those people were right.

You see, this woman just wanted to have a super slutty phase after a bad breakup. She wasn't looking for anything serious or long-term. And this dude just wanted to get back into the dating scene after a two-year hiatus while he actually dealt with his personal issues instead of making them a random girlfriend's problem. She was shockingly good at vegan junk food and personal finance advice, he was a man who could literally clean his own house and feed himself. Can I make it any more obvious? (That's an Avril Lavigne reference, for the Gen Z kids in the back.)

All this is to say, and I know it sounds so trite and silly and annoying like it's coming from your Aunt Mildred, but relationships will happen when and how they happen, and when you go chasing one thing, something else usually falls smack into your lap. But Millennials are here to ruin your day once again, this time with the senseless and cold-blooded murder of good old-fashioned relationships.

From Going Steady to Hookup Culture

Back in the days of my first marriage, I smugly joked with a haughtiness unbecoming of my future self that the list of people

I'd slept with was my marriage license. Oh my God, Past Me, could you not slut-shame? While I didn't partake in the hookup game in college, or indeed throughout my twenties, I did end up casually dating around while waiting out the legal formalities of my second divorce. I needed to be wild and free for a second, and if a dude didn't pan out, I had no trouble telling him to lose my number.

I've come a long way since my self-slut-shaming days, and so has society as a whole (or so I keep optimistically telling myself). I like to think we're moving toward a more sex-positive future inclusive of everyone's sexuality and bodily autonomy. From the asexual spectrum to people with high sex drives, from polyamorous lovers to those who are happily monogamous, from sex workers to people who've taken a vow of celibacy as part of their calling.

Part of the way this sex-positive brave new world plays out is casual dating, friends with benefits, and hookup culture. These days, it's fairly common to have a few partners at a time while you figure out who you click with the best, or indeed if you find yourself compatible with any partners. And it's totally okay to just hang out with someone for a fun time while you enjoy being single. There's no rule that says you can only put your time and energy into relationships with long-term potential.

While casual dating is a completely legitimate way to spend your time, it turns out that Millennials aren't doing it as much as people think we are. In fact, Millennials are actually having less sex than older generations were at our age. In a 2016 study, *Sexual Inactivity During Young Adulthood Is More Common*

Among U.S. Millennials and iGen: Age, Period, and Cohort Effects on Having No Sexual Partners After Age 18 (a lengthy but very informative title), researchers found that Americans born in the 1980s and 1990s were more likely to report having no sexual partners as adults, compared to Americans of the preceding Generation X.[42] A closer look revealed that, among participants between the ages of twenty and twenty-four, more than twice as many Millennial participants had no sexual partners since age eighteen as did Generation X participants. Learning this information made me feel like a sexual Benjamin Button, having first had sex at age eighteen and never experiencing a gap of more than a few months at a time since.

If we're not hooking up and we're also not shacking up or knocking up, what are we up to? Is our lack of sex a result of the overbooked work schedules so we can afford rent, the absolute crushing certainty that an unplanned pregnancy has the potential to completely alter the trajectory of our lives, a change in our sexual education, or a combination of these and other factors? Do the words of the *Mean Girls* gym teacher echo in our collective Millennial heads, warning, "If you have sex, you will get pregnant and die"?

Online Dating Pros and Cons

Online dating apps are an increasingly popular way to find a new potential mate. You can pick up on some personality traits, see their personal style, and swipe left if they have that inexplicable country-boy photo holding up a giant bass they just caught. Nobody wants to see your fish, dude. Unless you're into fishing, in which case, I implore you to go find all these dudes who put fish pics on their dating profiles.

However, online dating can also cause total burnout on dating and socializing. There's a lot of energy that goes into evaluating potential partners, establishing mutual interest, having a conversation, setting up a first date, and then hoping they're actually as nice as they seemed online. Online daters can also run into something akin to paralysis of choice—there are too many apps, too many people, too many messages to keep track of, and in this world of hustle and now and go for it, sometimes it feels easier to just lose the phone in the couch cushions for the evening and finish watching the latest season of *Jane the Virgin*.

This isn't even considering the risks of dating, emotional and physical. Without even touching on the sad state of sexism worldwide, the United States is a place rife with violence against women and sexual minorities, and there are many cases of women being attacked or murdered by men who became enraged when the women rejected their advances. As admitted sexual predator Louis C.K. put it, "How do women still go out with guys, when you consider the fact that there is *no* greater threat to women than men? We're the number one threat! To women! Globally and historically, we're the number one cause of injury and mayhem to women. We're the worst thing that ever happens to them! If you're a guy, imagine you could only date a half-bear-half-lion. 'Oh, I hope this one's nice!'"

What makes men the half-bear-half-lions of the modern dating world, and is there a way to check for the nice ones?

Smashing the Patriarchy

In order to talk about why men are so dangerous to women, we'll need to talk about everyone's favorite P-word: patriarchy. Inherent white patriarchal systems at play throughout history and still today are what support the marginalization of women, LGBT individuals, children, and basically everyone who isn't a cisgender heterosexual white dude.

This isn't just about glass ceilings or making seventy-seven cents per dollar a man makes for the same work (which is only true for white women, by the way—women of color make far less).[43] It's not about slut-shaming or the utter lack of functional pockets in women's clothing. It's not about expecting a hot dinner on the table when you walk in from work in the evening. It's about all of those things at once, plus the fact that *if you don't move out of a guy's way while you're walking toward each other, he will run into you because he expects you to have moved.* It's about every little thing like that, showing just how much women are expected to defer to men.

You can't talk about patriarchy without exploring the concept of toxic masculinity. This phrase, despite the snarky Facebook commentary from broflakes who can't handle criticism, does not mean that all men are toxic. It means that the way our society raises and conditions men to behave is toxic. "Boys don't cry" is toxic masculinity, training boys and men to not process their emotions. "Boys will be boys" is toxic masculinity, teaching boys that they don't have to be accountable for their actions because they are inherently rougher, tougher, and stronger than the girls. These two adages combined lead to entitled men who don't know how to express their emotions in any way but anger, because anger is strength. Anger is manly. Manly is good.

Little boys are shamed and manipulated away from doing things that appear too feminine, like painting their nails, taking dance classes, playing with dolls, or learning to cook. And this is the beautiful, wonderful thing about feminism—it's not about women being superior to men. It's about not shaming femininity or femaleness, which in turn would allow our young boys to gain emotional intelligence and be supported in any play or self-expression they want, thus reducing male anger and violent tendencies toward the world in adulthood. More emotionally intelligent children growing into secure adults means more emotional competency in the dating pool. Emotional intelligence is healthy.

If you doubt that masculinity is actively oppressing women in 2018, I suggest you ask the first man you find on the street and ask him if he's ever been the subject of a woman who was overly feminist. You see, this is a trick question, because there is no "overly feminist." Feminism seeks to provide the same level of agency and empowerment to every person regardless of gender. But I'd imagine over half of those men would tell a story about a time a girlfriend, friend, stranger on the subway, sister, etc., crossed the line and personally attacked him with feminist rhetoric. This attack nearly always turns out to be something involving the guy being publicly held accountable for saying or doing something douchey and sexist.

And while we're here, let's talk about everyone's favorite personal hell, the Friend Zone. The Friend Zone is a mythological holding cell in which women place men they want to be "just friends" with, usually while dating other men who treat them poorly. The nice guys in the Friend Zone just want to be there for their "friends" and are devastated by the fact that their targets—I mean, friends—are focusing their energy on other men.

Spoiler alert: the Friend Zone isn't a thing. If you have a friendship with someone, you are friends. Friendship is a reciprocal relationship built on commitment and emotional intimacy. If you want to add passion and hot sexy times to the friendship, talk to your friend, who retains the right at all times to opt not to participate in said sexy times with you, because she doesn't have to want something just because you do. And if she chooses not to pursue a sexual relationship with you, recognize that this choice is valid. If you get mad when somebody won't have sex with you, you're not friend-zoned, you're just an asshole.

Move Over, Monogamy

In recent years it seems like there's been an explosion of polyamorous resources and support groups. People "come out" as polyamorous after grappling with the fact that their friends and family may find their lack of monogamy to be a moral failing. But who says we must only be with one person at a time?

As outlined in *Stepping Off the Relationship Escalator: Uncommon Love and Life* by Amy Gahran, "traditional" relationships follow a pretty standard and common theme, advancing along societally agreed upon status points.[44] First comes the initial flirtation and casual dating, then labeling or "claiming" one another as a couple, using terms like partner or boyfriend. At this point, you're on the escalator toward an established and committed long-term relationship, and this is where the popular, "So where's this relationship going, what are we?" conversation comes in. Once you're on the escalator, you typically progress through merging households, marrying, and having a family.

This progression is completely valid and fulfilling for a great many people. But it's not for everyone, and Millennials appear to be more open to nontraditional variants of the escalator approach.

When I left my second marriage, which had been emotionally and psychologically abusive, I committed to having a year without monogamy. I could not dare to fall into the trap of being charmed and controlled again, and I knew that deliberately keeping myself from a monogamous, committed relationship was one way to hack my brain into keeping my boundaries front and center, to notice and deal with red flags. In the past, I'd be so happy to find someone I clicked with that I would overlook obvious warning signs in the hope that it would all work out. Because fate, or whatever.

In the two weeks after I moved out of my former husband's house, I went on a handful of first dates and, yes, had some casual sex. One guy in particular stands out as a shining example of my new boundaries. After a date that went exceptionally well, we went our separate ways, and then later that night we were texting, and I invited him over. Things progressed as things sometimes do when you text a guy to come over at night, and the next morning I awoke to a couple visible hickeys on my neck. I texted him a simple, "Hey, I had a great time, but I don't appreciate being marked without asking first." Enter his mansplaining excuses about how it was because he didn't think my skin was so sensitive (it's not) and that he kept doing it because I was "responding to said stimulus." The more we were talking about this, the more I felt myself feeling distant and a little panicky, my heart was racing, and I was starting to feel a fight or flight response. I realized I was having an anxiety attack and that he was speaking to me the way my ex did, explaining why I was actually the reason behind the thing that upset me. I told him I wasn't feeling it and wished him good luck. That was that. (PS: This is an example of subtle gaslighting.)

Since my initial two-week swipe fest, I've been happily non-monogamous with two partners. And wouldn't you know, we can have healthy conversations about boundaries and trauma responses, and everyone is a competent adult about it.

When introducing polyamory as a concept to most people, their initial response is something along the lines of "Well, isn't that just cheating with permission?" and other questions about possession and jealousy. And these are topics that absolutely should be addressed in any non-monogamous relationship, especially if the relationship begins on the traditional monogamous track and is opened up later. In my case, I went into both my relationships completely honest with my partners about my stance on monogamy, so there have been few issues, if any, around jealousy.

An eye-opening introduction to the concept of polyamory and personal autonomy is the book *More Than Two,* by Franklin

Veaux and Eve Rickert. In their book and on its accompanying website, they outline what they call the Relationship Bill of Rights. Included in this Bill of Rights are the rights to choose the level of intimacy you want, to revoke consent, to communicate your emotions and needs, to seek balance between the give and take of your relationships, to make mistakes, and to end a relationship.[45]

The idea that you have not only the ability, but the *right*, to end a relationship or revoke consent at any time for any form of intimacy, are concepts not commonly celebrated in our society. It seems that in any breakup, there needs to be a villain and a victim, a winner and a loser. But honestly, it's okay to simply realize you and your partner just aren't working out for whatever reason, and step away.

I once ended a brief relationship, and the breakup was absolutely devastating to my partner. It was awful to feel okay about it on my end while seeing how upset she was, but I still knew that it was the right thing for me to do. And it wasn't necessarily anyone's fault, more of a combination of factors like communication, distance, and a mismatch of intensity levels and expectations about the relationship. But it was important for me to stand firm on my boundaries and remember the Relationship Bill of Rights and the fact that I had the right to change my mind and end our relationship.

Polyamory is not without challenges and negatives, but neither is monogamy. Neither one is a magic bullet to solve communication issues, intimacy needs, or jealousy concerns, and both approaches to relationships are valid. Whether monogamous or not, however, it's important to remember that relationships aren't just a trip up the escalator, to a happily-ever-after dictated by society's (or your own) expectations. Relationships involve two or more people with their own emotions, boundaries, past traumas, and needs.

The truth is, no one owes you any part of themselves. Relationships should be freely entered and involve respect for each partner's autonomy.

Relationship Anarchy

I swear, I'm not just making stuff up. Relationship anarchy, often abbreviated RA (not to be confused with rheumatoid arthritis or your college resident assistant), is a relationship framework that basically says, do what you want, with whomever you want, and don't be a dick about it.

Relationship anarchy eschews the possession and ownership models of relationships that echo back into our collective unconscious from the time when a women would be transferred from father to husband along with the thanks of a few hearty milk goats or camels for taking her off Dad's hands. According to Wikipedia, keeper of all knowledge, RA "is the belief that relationships should not be bound by rules aside from what the people involved mutually agree upon." Furthermore, relationship anarchy does not distinguish between levels of relationship and includes platonic friendships, sexual relationships, romantic relationships, and anything in between. It equalizes all forms of intimacy as important to the people in the relationship. Many relationship anarchists don't use labels or categorize their relationships as dating, open, platonic, etc.—they simply exist within each individual relationship, without rank or hierarchy.

While on the surface this approach seems to fly in the face of what we've all been taught is normal, a deeper look tends to be somewhat refreshing. The idea that your close friendships are just as important as romantic ones is something we are not inherently taught in our upbringing, and many people tend to lose friendships when they focus on a new love interest or partner. But the RA model allows people to prioritize all relationships equally, and through this re-learning, we can realize that we're the ones in charge of who we spend our time with. Nobody owns our time, our intimacy, or our emotional capacity.

Relationship anarchy also dovetails with the rejection of heteronormative and monogamous expectations, as well as norms around family. Why is it so weird for two friends to move in together to raise their kids? Why is it abnormal for people to share the holidays with friends instead of relatives? Because these things reject the basic concepts that people should stay close with their family of origin, go up a relationship escalator, procreate in a married or otherwise committed relationship, and repeat.

It's totally okay to move in with your bestie and raise your kids together. That family sounds awesome. Imagine being raised by two people who love and support each other, without romance. What could children learn from seeing healthy friendship and support modeled from day one? There is more to life than finding a romantic partner to love until you die. Live your life. Love everyone you love. Don't subscribe to what romantic comedies tell you is the ideal. Fuck all that noise.

How to Make Sure You're Killing It

You Define Your Relationships. And by that, I mean that you're in charge of defining, or not defining, the relationships you want to be in, your level of intimacy in those relationships, and your expectations in those relationships. This goes for all relationships, whether sexual, romantic, platonic, or otherwise.

Practice Safer Sex. You and your sexual partners should screen for sexually transmitted infections regularly (at least annually). If you have multiple partners, aim for twice a year. Definitely get tested if you plan to have unprotected sex with a partner. There's still a stigma around being tested for STIs, as if the testing itself indicates that you're a risky partner. News flash, every time you have sex there's a risk of infection or pregnancy. Safer sex is all about reducing risks. Barrier methods, birth control, and regular STI screenings are all about risk reduction, which keeps everyone a little safer.

You Don't Owe Anybody Anything. Sex and relationships are not transactional. Relationships are about consent, whether that's consenting to a date in the first place, consenting to sex, or even consenting to a hug or goodnight kiss. You get to change your mind at any time. I was once messaging with a guy on an app and told him that I do a platonic coffee date first before anything else happens, and he asked me several times if sex was on the table for the first date. When I pointed out that I had already said no to sex on the coffee date and he continued to push the boundary, he acted like I was being unreasonable and condescending. Block people who don't understand the word no.

Nobody Owes You Anything. Aha, the other side! Everyone gets to say no, change their mind, or just not be interested—even to you. There is no punch card that means if you're nice to somebody ten times, you get a kiss or a sexual favor. Be respectful of people's choices and decisions. Respect will get you a lot further than cranky temper tantrums because you don't get what you want.

Get Enthusiastic Consent. Somehow our sex education leaves a lot out about the concept of consent. Consent is not a boring interruption to the mood while you haltingly ask if your partner would like to indeed have some sex. Consent should be enthusiastic and without gray areas or anything "subject to interpretation." A partner saying "Yeah, sure, I guess we can have sex" is not enthusiastic consent. A partner saying, "I'm fine, let's do it," while upset or giving nonverbal cues of discomfort is not enthusiastic consent. And so on and so forth. If this concept confuses you or makes you feel that getting enthusiastic consent is too much work, take a break from dating for a year and figure that shit out.

There is No Timeline. You do not have to rush, you do not have to take your time, you do not have to meet certain criteria, and you do not have to get things out of the way before you commit. Basically, there's no prescriptive way to go about dating, relationships, or raising a family. I have single friends who don't plan to have children, friends in relationships who don't plan to have children, single friends with kids, etc. You get the picture. When I was married, we tried for over a year to get pregnant. I was distraught every month, and I was so stressed about not becoming a mother by age thirty when I had wanted to have my

THE GASLIGHTING OF THE MILLENNIAL GENERATION

first baby. When I left that marriage, I went from moving out of our house to meeting a serious boyfriend in about two weeks. I resisted it, made sure we limited our contact, cut back on dates and communication, all because I felt like it was too soon to be having feelings for someone before I'd had time to fully heal from an abusive relationship. It took my sister and a close friend telling me that there's no timeline for healing or for love to make me realize it was okay to just let the chips fall where they may.

Know the Signs of Emotional Abuse. It takes survivors an average of seven attempts to leave an abusive relationship. So many people ask, "Why did they stay if it was so bad?" without understanding what is truly at play in abusive situations. Oftentimes the abuser gains control slowly over time and may gain or maintain control through financial, emotional, and psychological abuse that causes the survivor to doubt their own perceptions of how bad it is; sometimes an abuser will use sexual abuse, resulting in pregnancy, to keep the victim dependent on the abuser for survival or resources. Whether you are single or in a relationship, I implore you spend an hour on the domestic violence hotline website to get to know signs of abuse in relationships.

Trust Your Gut. If something seems off, it's okay to call it quits.

Manage Expectations. When you start sharing your life with someone else, whether it's happy hour once in a while or regular weekends at each other's place or being married, there are expectations at play. And expectations (or rather, unmet expectations) are one of the quickest ways to breed resentment and create conflict in a relationship. If you expect your partner to discuss any dates with other people because you're not in a monogamous relationship, tell them. If you expect your partner to split the driving and alternate date locations because you live an hour apart, tell them. If you expect your partner to not eat dairy on nights they sleep over because it makes them gassy and their farts keep you up all night, tell them. Otherwise you'll just be mad all the time, and that is zero fun.

Handle Your Emotional Labor. This one is mostly for the cis dudes who complain that they can't even have a conversation or give a woman a compliment these days because women think everything is sexual harassment. Have you ever stopped to consider that you may, in fact, be harassing someone? Educate yourself instead of relying on the women in your life to point out that you're behaving like a misogynist. Also, if you need an emotional outlet, romantic partners are a good part of your support network, but they are not your entire support network. Spread your emotional needs out between friends, family, partners, and a trusted therapist, so that you're not putting all of your needs into one person's basket and making them personally responsible for your mental wellbeing. This sucks; please don't do it.

It Happens When You Least Expect It. I know, it's so corny! But it's super for real. Quit trying so hard to find "the one" or look for signs or connections or messages from the Universe. Just live your life, run like hell toward what makes you feel amazing and incredible and like you are living your best life. If you're running headlong into your authentic life, and not trying to find a soul mate in every rando who comes across your Tinder app, you'll naturally attract the kind of partners who will complement your lifestyle and passions.

Love Yourself. This isn't one of those "Love yourself in order to truly love another" things because you're worthy of love even if you aren't loving yourself right now. But maybe, just maybe, you could add some mindfulness and self-compassion to your routine, so that you can work on living that best life for someone else to complement.

Get Tested. I know I already said this, but seriously.

Chapter 11

Millennials Are Killing Parenting

*"15 Stats About Millennial Moms That
Will Make You Feel Like Garbage"*

—Baby Gaga, May 2017

*"Millennials may be history's most
competent parents. Here's why."*

—Winnie.com, September 2017

I always planned to have a baby by age thirty. When I first got married at age twenty-one, I assumed we'd eventually start planning to have a family. We divorced before that was ever on the table. When I was twenty-five, I made a five-year plan to be pregnant by thirty. And when I got married again at age twenty-eight, we started trying for a baby right away. My husband was over seventeen years my senior and wasn't getting any younger, so we skipped the newlywed "Just enjoy each life without kids" advice because we'd been together for over five years at this point and we were ready to start a family. Only it never happened. We were trying to conceive for over eighteen months. Eighteen times, I filled the bathroom trash can with a layer of negative pregnancy tests. Eighteen times, I had to find a sexy way to say, "Hey, I'm ovulating, let's do this."

In retrospect, I'm beyond thankful that we never got pregnant, because then I'd have to see my ex-husband every other weekend for far too long and that would suck. Now I'm two divorces deep into adulthood, still childless, still making cute faces at babies who wander across my path, and still excited about parenting, someday. At the same time, I've spent enough time with my friends and their kids to know that I'm still in that sweet spot of only being accountable to and responsible for myself alone, and I don't have to grow, nourish, and raise any other humans. Despite all the heartbreak and frustration for nearly two years, when I wanted a baby so badly and was arguably doing everything right to make that dream come true, I'm glad I have another five-year plan of just working on me and doing the things I need to do to grow, nourish, and raise myself.

I am still undecided about my plans to have children, biological or otherwise. I'm realizing that just because I think I'd be good at something doesn't mean I have to do it. Whatever I decide at the end of this new five year plan, I've learned a lot about the type of parent I'd want to be.

Why Millennials Are Parenting Differently

Back in the Boomer days, B.G. (Before Google), when young adults had children, they largely had only a few resources and role models to guide their parenting questions: their own parents, their doctors, and their community. Maybe some books or newspaper articles. The village was supportive, but somewhat of an echo chamber. But now, the village is online, y'all. Curious about sleep regressions, growth spurts, teething, why your nipples hurt so bad, or a recipe for lactation cookies? Need to get recommendations for the best no-spill sippy cup or baby thermometer or where to find that damn Sophie the Giraffe teether?

Enter Google. Basically, everything you could ever have a question about has an answer online. Parents today can access help and find resources faster and more effectively than generations past. We no longer have to rely on "Well, my parents did it this way, so it's good enough for me," when we can find support online for doing things differently.

And we are definitely doing things differently than our parents did.

Back to Basics

It's interesting to note that many of the so-called "Millennial" parenting trends that are gaining traction are actually not new or unique to our generation at all. Attachment parenting, more common among Millennials than older generations, involves a foundation of secure attachment between parent and child. For many parents, this means bedsharing, nursing, babywearing, and other means of keeping baby close—but these aren't new phenomena, nor are they unique to the United States.

The benefits of attachment parenting are varied. There's an obvious cost savings when using reusable, washable cloth diapers over disposables, and there's also a reduction in waste and a family's carbon footprint (for those of us who are concerned eco-freaks). Plus, cloth diapers are adorable, people. Bedsharing and co-sleeping correlates to a reduced risk of Sudden Infant Death Syndrome (SIDS) and helps foster secure attachment. It's also way more convenient for nursing parents to handle nighttime feedings, when they can just sleepily insert a boob into a fussy baby's mouth for meal time. Nursing is also a convenient and cost-reductive way to keep baby fed: you never have to worry about running out of formula, or having a bottle of water, etc., when you feed straight from the tap. Although your grocery bill will go up a little because you will need to eat constantly, thanks to the calorie burn of nursing.

This isn't to say that Millennial parents don't use disposable diapers or strollers or formula. Many parents cannot or do not want to feed their children via nursing, which is a valid choice. However, the health benefits of breastfeeding are innumerable and include a reduced risk of asthma and allergies, fewer ear infections and respiratory illnesses, and an overall better immune system thanks to the antibodies found naturally in breast milk (which change based on baby's needs—the human body is an absolute wonder). Some nursing parents have to exclusively pump, supplement by pumping, or even rely on donated milk entirely due to schedule constraints, necessary medications not compatible with nursing, or physical obstacles to nursing such as inverted nipples, insufficient glandular tissue, and tongue or lip ties that prevent baby from successfully latching.

Wow, that was a lot of talking about breasts in the middle of this book about Millennials smashing the patriarchy and stuff. Let's make sure we're still on track. Are Millennials nursing more than their parents did? Indeed, they are. In a 2013 press release, the CDC reported that babies breastfeeding at six months had increased from 35 percent in 2000 to 49 percent in 2010.[46] Babies still nursing at one year of age had also increased from 15 percent in 2000 to 27 percent in 2010.

Millennial parents are choosing to parent differently than they were raised. Subjectively, this speaks to a societal shift and a generational declaration of "I won't raise my children the way I was raised." Millennials are cautious parents in this new age of cyber bullying and people calling Child Protective Services for kids playing outside, but they're not controlling parents. What else is different between generations?

Millennial Discipline

"Stop crying or I'll give you something to cry about."

"Stop crying or I won't take you to be in your school play tomorrow night."

These are two literal quotes from my own childhood. I wasn't spanked a lot, but I do remember a few moments of physical punishment, often after a stern count to three. These days, we've got scientific evidence confirming that spanking and physical punishment leads to lasting damage in children and adults. Additionally, spanking doesn't even *work* the way people think it should.

In a comprehensive study entitled "Spanking and child outcomes: Old controversies and new meta-analyses," researchers explored fifty years of research on spanking involving over 160,000 children.[47] The results indicated that spanking is ineffective (more spanking leads to more defiance) and damaging (spanking correlates with anti-social behavior, aggression, cognitive difficulties, and mental health issues). This meta-analysis specifically focused on disciplinary spanking, defined as an open-handed strike on extremities or the child's buttocks, not "potentially abusive behaviors." In other words, the analysis centered around the basic swat on the ass to get your kids to listen to you and behave better.

Spoiler alert: spanking doesn't work.

Research found that disciplinary spanking correlates with the same negative outcomes as child abuse, though to a slightly lesser degree. Hopping back to the data on Adverse Childhood Experiences, or ACEs, from Chapter 2, abuse (including psychological, physical, and sexual) and household dysfunction (including substance abuse, mental illness, violence, and criminal behavior) result in multiple negative outcomes. The outcomes correlated with ACEs include smoking, substance abuse, obesity, depression, and suicide attempts. Such adverse outcomes are only slightly less prevalent in children from non-abusive homes that used spanking as a punishment.

The Millennial parent is more likely to practice gentle discipline, encouraging deep breaths, calm comfort, and using words to communicate through tantrums rather than using physical punishments to control behavior. There's a flowchart floating around the internet about whether or not to spank a child. It begins, "Is the child old enough to understand reason?" A yes response leads to, "Use reason." A no response leads to, "Then they aren't old enough to understand why you're spanking." This is really the simplest way to put it, and showcases the fact that spanking is an ineffective way to handle discipline. Striking another person, regardless of their age, gender, or the reason behind the strike, is an inherently violent action and produces a lasting impact on the brain, especially in the developmental years of childhood.

The Millennial parent is more open-minded and open to new information. Just as there are many different types and styles of families, there are many different types and styles of parenting methods. Gentle parenting methods seek to communicate and support, rather than demand obedience. The gentle Millennial parent tries to understand the cause of a child's "poor behavior," usually related to a need the child has. When a baby, toddler, or even older child is hungry, tired, overstimulated, scared, or angry, they display cues that parents can learn to interpret. Meltdowns and tantrums are nearly always related to an unmet need. Whether or not your tired toddler actually settles down for a nap is another story, but on the whole, gentle parents find that, if they can at least understand why a child is melting down, they can meet the child with understanding instead of demands to stop crying or face a harsh punishment.

Diverging from How Mom Did It

One of the things I absolutely adore about this generation is that we have no qualms about looking at advice or behavior from our parents and giving it a hearty, "No thanks, actually." As we experience the cultural awakening that we don't actually have to do what people expect us to do, and we're responsible for our own damn selves, we have the confidence to distance ourselves from the way we were raised or told to do things.

For example, when I learned how wholly unnecessary and dangerous routine infant circumcision was, I was appalled. I had just assumed that everyone did it, that it was done for a legitimate reason, and that it made sense. As it turns out, routine circumcision of infants leads to over a hundred deaths per year due to blood loss and other complications, it is extremely painful and causes babies to go into shock, and it causes loss of sensation in the penis throughout life. It doesn't even offer any benefits or reasonable items for the "pro" column.

THE GASLIGHTING OF THE MILLENNIAL GENERATION

When I presented this information to my mother, back when I still ran every piece of thought process by her, hoping for a nugget of validation, she fought back. "Well, I circumcised both your brothers. It's cleaner." I naturally retorted with my research and data, indicating the risks and fallacies around how "clean" circumcision is. First off, it's an open wound in a diaper, that doesn't sound great to me. Secondly, there's no special cleaning required for intact penises. You just wash your body like normal. Thirdly, believing that boys and men aren't capable of cleaning their own penises is sort of bullshit. Bonus fourth item, if it's not your penis and there's not a health concern that requires surgical intervention, hands off! Consent and bodily autonomy, people. It's not that difficult.

Alright, I got off on a tangent there (because I really believe people should research this stuff before they subject their kids to it), but I told you that story to point out how my mom wouldn't even entertain the idea that she did something less than perfect or okay. To the point that she ignored scientific data, she would not admit that maybe the way she did things wasn't the best option.

As a generation of people who don't obligate themselves to their parents just for birthing them, this can be tricky to navigate. Because Boomer parents have a hard time accepting that you might do something differently, they feel judged and might push back. Hold your ground and stick to the decisions you feel are best for your family, while remaining open to legitimate disagreements that might help inform your decisions in the future.

The Millennial parent does not stick their head in the sand. They learn, they ask advice from their friends about their own experiences, they look to research and data, and they are willing to change their minds if presented with evidence. On the whole, Millennials tend to own their shortcomings fairly well, no matter how much the Boomers whine that we're entitled crybabies who can't take criticism. Try being constructive with it, Boomers, and take some yourself!

How to Make Sure You're Killing It

Taking advice from a childless author on how to kill it at this parenting thing is, I know, not the most credible thing in the world. But you are taking (or at least reading) the advice of a childless author who has spent over six years researching conception, pregnancy, childbirth, and early childrearing in preparation to have a baby. I do know some stuff, even if I've never put it into practice yet.

Know That It's Okay to Have Preferences. Internet trolls will try to shame you for having a birth plan, or wanting to use a doula, or going for an unmedicated birth. These people are not important. Your desires are important. You are allowed to want these things, and you are allowed to prepare for the birth and parenting experience you want.

Know That Sometimes Things Don't Go According to Plan. It is definitely okay to prepare for the experience you want, but it's also a good idea to stay open-minded about a backup plan. Lots of parents plan to breastfeed their babies, or plan to breastfeed for a certain length of time, but they end up with a nursing issue or need to wean early. That's okay, and things not going according to plan doesn't make you a bad parent or a failure.

Screen Time is Okay. Yeah, screens can mess with your sleep. But screens can also keep your kid busy when you need five dang minutes. Or an hour. I'm not judging.

It's Okay to Not Have Kids. If you're childless by choice, you probably skipped this chapter, but if you're still here, you are totally valid! Not everyone needs to have kids. Not everyone wants to have kids. If you don't want children, that is fine. Don't let your Aunt Edna shame you for being selfish. You live your life. You do not owe the world 2.2 kids.

Your Family Size is No One's Business. Similar to the point above, if you want to have zero kids, that's fine. If you want one kid, two kid, red kid, blue kid, that's fine. If you have a surprise sixth baby and people give you the side eye in the grocery store, pay them no mind, because it's not their business.

Social Support is Key. The Millennial Generation is bringing back the village, or at least they're trying to. Whether you can rely on nearby friends for playdates or just getting out of the house for sanity, you can plop your kids into once-a-week day care, or you're seeing a therapist for some human interaction and to make sure your own needs don't get lost in the struggle, build a robust social support network.

Be Aware of Postpartum Depression. Depression, anxiety, psychosis, even OCD can come along postpartum and knock you on your ass. And it's not just the parents who bear the children, even non-birthing parents can be affected by postpartum disorders. Be aware of the signs, and do not be afraid to get help.

Every Kid is Different. Beware the easy first child, who will make you believe having babies is easy and effortless. This is a trick designed by nature to make you have another baby who will pull your hair and never sleep. Hyperbole aside, each kid really is different! They'll have different needs and preferences. Some will want to snuggle all the time and others will learn to walk and run away from you at every chance.

Stay at Home—Or Don't. Even if you want to be a stay-at-home parent with every fiber of your being, it might drive you nuts. And even if you plan to go back to work after maternity leave, you may change your mind when you're home with baby. Either option, or any option in between, is acceptable. Remember, if someone isn't paying your bills, their opinion doesn't matter! If you want to stay home, weigh the cost of commuting and day care against your salary, and if you can take the financial hit, do it. Staying at home is valid. Going back to work is valid.

It Goes Fast. Of all the advice that new parents roll their eyes at, "Enjoy it now, it goes fast!" is probably the worst. Do not say this to a mom holding a toddler in meltdown mode at Target. It will not help her. But honestly, y'all, it goes fast. It goes so fast. Breathe in their little baby scents, snuggle when they want to snuggle, even when you just want to eat your peanut butter cup in peace, wash the pair of pajamas they have to wear right now tonight or else they'll die...because it goes fast. And they'll remember every time you were there for them.

Chapter 12

Millennials Are Killing the Blame Game

"Move Over, Millennials, Here Comes Generation Z"

—*The New York Times*, September 2015

After eleven chapters of patriarchy-smashing, sanity-validating, done-with-all-this-bullshit breakdowns of how Millennials are dismantling society for the good of the next generations, there's still some work to do to make sure we don't get tired of our changemaking and lay the blame at the feet of our children like our own elders did.

I intend this book to be a call to arms to my Millennial peers, young and old. Do not stop fighting. Do not stop calling out the problems you see. Do not stop working for change. And do not point the finger at the next generation and make the same mistakes.

We see the ways our society has wronged us. We see the ways they blame us for things gone sideways when they were always going to go sideways. We see survivors of abuse and harassment. We see each other. We believe each other.

Just like anyone who has experienced abuse and gaslighting, we have a choice to make. We can say, "I suffered, why shouldn't they?" Or we can say, "I suffered, and it was some bullshit, and I'm going to do my best to make sure it doesn't happen again." I implore you to choose the latter.

I've seen countless people within the Millennial generation describes themselves as "definitely not a Millennial," because they want to distance themselves from the negative stereotypes. They want to be "not like other girls" on a generational level. But here's the thing: there are two definitions of Millennial. One definition is based in solid and immutable facts, that Millennials were born between 1980 and 2000 in a twenty-year cohort of census and social data. The other definition lives and breathes. It's what makes so many of us claim the name Millennial to mean more than birth years, more than stereotypes, and more than a scoff of disbelief that we'd dare to be different.

Millennial means you care, it means you get up in the morning even when it's hard, it means you have seen the way you and your friends are treated in this world and you said, "Wait, this shouldn't be this hard." Millennial is a kinship among those like us and those who can sum up their exhaustion and struggle with the one-word label that defines our birth years.

Millennial is a battle cry and call to arms. It is forming a human chain of solidarity and support. Of belief and validation. Of wanting to do better and leave a better world for those who come next. It is I hear you and I believe you and I will go with you and me too.

Millennial is amazing.

And Gen Z, or the iGeneration, or whatever they end up being called by themselves or society, is amazing. The kids these days are already experiencing the same stresses we are, at younger and younger ages. One of my closest friends is a teacher, and she called me heartbroken one day to tell me a story of her student who said, "I have to do well in school while I'm trying to deal with all of these feelings and it's so hard." This student is in third grade. Everything is about achievement, performance, and bottom lines, so much so that we never learned to just be, and we're not teaching the next generation how to just be, either. Kids need to play, they need time to sleep and grow, they need the space and safety to feel their feelings and be vulnerable. This same teacher was told not to cry in a meeting with her principal and that she didn't have the luxury of being stressed or panicked at work. The message is clear: "Leave your personal life at home, you're here to work," and we are uniquely positioned to throw this message in the garbage as we change the landscape of the workforce and our society at large.

Millennials are huge. We have enormous buying power in the marketplace (after all, we're killing industries left and right, remember?). We have jobs. We have families. We don't put up with mistreatment. We demand better. And holy shit, do we demand better for our kids.

After being raised to doubt ourselves and our value, we stand up with so much self-worth and so many boundaries that the Boomers are rightly quaking in their boots. And it's our turn to influence the way things go now. We must raise up the next society of children to never have to doubt that they are loved and that their thoughts and feelings are valid. We can and should support them and listen to them like we wish those in our childhoods had listened to us. We can finally be the adults we needed when we were younger.

How to Make Sure You're Killing It

Check yourself before you complain about the youth. If you catch yourself thinking, "Oh my God, these kids are so blah blah blah," imagine your parents saying it about you, and if it makes you mad, don't say it. Remember that all the old white dudes want you to be mad at the kids and not them.

Be compassionate. Young people are in the unique position of having to learn how to exist in the world while being expected to already know how to do it. (Of course, I'm still struggling with this in my thirties, but whatever.) It is hard to be a teenager. You're full of hormones and trying to figure out what to do with your life and probably have a part-time job and you have all this pressure to do well in school and you're probably also in some clubs or sports and maybe you have to go pick up your little sister from school on the way home. It's a lot! If you have teenagers, or you know teenagers, cut them some slack and be supportive and compassionate, instead of giving them the ol' "Back in my day" spiel.

Use your privilege. Most people forget that a lot of "those darn Millennials" are well into their thirties now, existing in society all sneaky-like. Use your status as a Respected Human Adult to make the noise the younger Millennials and Gen Z kids can't, because they'll be ignored. You won't be ignored, especially if you have additional privileges of race or gender (looking at you, Millennial white dudes).

Raise your kids to understand consent and feelings. Teach them it's not okay to invade people's personal space or act like a jerk.

Tell them it's okay to not have their shit together. Seriously. The secret of life is that you really never have it all together.

About the Author

Caitlin Fisher wanted a witty caption
but couldn't think of anything before her deadline.
She hopes you have an awesome day.

Caitlin Fisher wrote her first book when she was six, a self-illustrated autobiography in pencil and crayon. She never expected to publish a real book, but her life has always brought her back to the written word, no matter what her professional position. As an undergraduate student, she wrote for the school newspaper and relished in research papers for psychology courses, and with a master's degree in Higher Education Administration she planned to become a professional career counselor for students, assisting with cover letters and resumes.

With fifty thousand dollars in student loan debt and zero job prospects, she temped at a real estate office in her hometown before landing a full-time position as a specialty chemical purchaser, which had nothing at all to do with her educational background. After nearly four years building a freelance copywriting business, she made the leap into full-time marketing copywriting and is now a marketing content manager for an Ohio greenhouse.

In 2012, facing the packed-up cardboard aftermath of a divorce, she downsized and started a blog, *Born Again Minimalist*. Over the years, this website changed from a focus on *less stuff* to a focus on *more self-advocacy*. In 2016, Fisher accidentally went viral. A blog post with a scathing message, that her entire generation had been set up to fail as a massive generational scapegoat, struck a chord with readers. It is this blog post that served as the inspiration and starting point for *The Gaslighting of the Millennial Generation* published in 2019. Fisher is a burned-out thirty-something who cannot abide for a single moment that her peers might turn around and do this to the next generation.

This book is a call to action: It stops here. We change now. Or else.

Caitlin Fisher lives in the Highland Square neighborhood of Akron, Ohio with a partner, an elderly cat, and ten houseplants. She lives her own advice and has spent the last two years establishing boundaries, understanding her value and worth, and not backing down.

Reach Caitlin via her website at www.caitlinfisherauthor. com, Instagram @caitlinfisherauthor, or on Facebook.com/ CaitlinFisherAuthor.

Endnotes

1   "The Millennial Generation Research Review." US Chamber of Commerce Foundation. November 12, 2012. Accessed 2016. https://www.uschamberfoundation.org/reports/millennial-generation-research-review.

2   Russell, Cheryl. *The Baby Boom*. 8th ed. The American Generations. East Patchogue, NY: New Strategist Press LLC, 2015. Online excerpt accessed 2018. http://www.newstrategist.com/wp-content/uploads/2017/01/BB8.SamplePgs.pdf

3   Steverman, Ben. "Americans Are Dying Faster. Millennials, Too." Bloomberg. October 28, 2016. Accessed 2017. https://www.bloomberg.com/news/articles/2016-10-28/americans-are-dying-faster-millennials-too.

4   Holder, Josh, Paul Torpey, and Feilding Cage. "How Does the US Healthcare System Compare with Other Countries?" July 25, 2017. Accessed 2018. https://www.theguardian.com/us-news/ng-interactive/2017/jul/25/us-healthcare-system-vs-other-countries.

5   Bichell, Rae Ellen. "Average Age of First-Time Moms Keeps Climbing in The U.S." NPR. January 14, 2016. Accessed 2018. https://www.npr.org/sections/health-shots/2016/01/14/462816458/average-age-of-first-time-moms-keeps-climbing-in-the-u-s.

6   Notte, Jason. "Millennials Have Redefined the American Dream." The Street. May 1, 2017. Accessed 2017. https://www.thestreet.com/story/14110114/1/millennials-have-redefined-the-american-dream.html.

7   Chopra, Krish. "Why Your Millennials Are Leaving (And How to Keep Them)." Forbes. March 23, 2018. Accessed December 2018. https://www.forbes.com/sites/theyec/2018/03/23/why-your-millennials-are-leaving-and-how-to-keep-them/amp/.

8   Caramela, Sammi. "How Companies Can Change Their Culture to Attract (and Retain) Millennials." Business.com. February 12, 2018. Accessed December 2018. https://www.business.com/articles/how-are-companies-changing-their-culture-to-attract-and-retain-millennials/.

9   Mann, Leslie. "How Family Members Cope with Estrangement." Chicago Tribune. July 3, 2017. Accessed December 2018. https://www.chicagotribune.com/lifestyles/sc-estrangement-from-family-0711-20170703-story,amp.html.

10 Moss, Gabrielle. "Not All Millennials Are Close to Their Parents, No Matter What Trend Pieces Tell You." Bustle. December 14, 2014. Accessed December 2018. https://www.bustle.com/articles/53777-not-all-millennials-are-close-to-their-parents-no-matter-what-trend-pieces-tell-you.

11 Howe, Neil, and William Strauss. *Millennials Rising: The Next Great Generation*. New York, NY: Vintage Books, 2000: p. 137.

12 Spertus, Ilyse L., Rachel Yehuda, Cheryl M. Wong, Sarah Halligan, and Stephanie V. Seremetis. "Childhood Emotional Abuse and Neglect as Predictors of Psychological and Physical Symptoms in Women Presenting to a Primary Care Practice." *Child Abuse & Neglect* 27, no. 11 (November 2003): 1247-1258. Accessed 2017. https://www.sciencedirect.com/journal/child-abuse-and-neglect/vol/27/issue/11.

13   Bierer, L. M., R. Yehuda, J. Schmeidler, V. Mitropoulou, A. S. New, J. M. Silverman, and
     L. J. Siever. "Abuse and Neglect in Childhood: Relationship to Personality Disorder
     Diagnoses." *CNS Spectrums* 8, no. 10 (October 2003): 737-754. Accessed 2017.
     https://www.ncbi.nlm.nih.gov/pubmed/14712172#.

14   Bodker, Ilana. "How Baby Boomer Parents Molded the Millennial Generation." Barkley.
     August 15, 2017. Accessed December 2018. https://www.barkleyus.com/insights/
     baby-boomer-parents-molded-millennial-generation/.

15   C. Bradley-Geist Jill B. Olson-Buchanan Julie. "Helicopter parents: an examination
     of the correlates of over-parenting of college students." Education + Training,
     Vol. 56 Issue 4 (2014): 314-328. Accessed 2017. https://www.researchgate.net/
     publication/263764668_Helicopter_parents_An_examination_of_the_correlates_of_
     over-parenting_of_college_students

16   Givertz, Michelle & Segrin, Chris. (2012). The Association Between Overinvolved
     Parenting and Young Adults' Self-Efficacy, Psychological Entitlement, and Family
     Communication. Communication Research. 41. 10.1177/0093650212456392.

17   Felitti, Vincent J., Robert F. Anda, Dale Nordenberg, David F. Williamson, Alison M.
     Spitz, Valerie Edwards, and James S. Marks. "Relationship of childhood abuse and
     household dysfunction to many of the leading causes of death in adults: The Adverse
     Childhood Experiences (ACE) Study." *American journal of preventive medicine* 14, no.
     4 (1998): 245-258.

18   "Millennials at Work." Bentley University. November 11, 2014. Accessed 2017. https://
     www.bentley.edu/newsroom/latest-headlines/mind-of-millennial.

19   Chew, Jonathan. "Why Millennials Would Take a $7,600 Pay Cut for a New Job."
     Fortune. April 8, 2016. Accessed January 2019. http://fortune.com/2016/04/08/
     fidelity-millennial-study-career/.

20   Schulte, Brigid. "Millennials Want a Work-life Balance. Their Bosses Just Don't Get
     Why." The Washington Post. May 5, 2015. Accessed January 2019. https://www.
     washingtonpost.com/local/millennials-want-a-work-life-balance-their-bosses-
     just-dont-get-why/2015/05/05/1859369e-f376-11e4-84a6-6d7c67c50db0_story.
     html?utm_term=.ab98ac6aa11a.

21   Schulte, Brigid. "Millennials Want a Work-life Balance. Their Bosses Just Don't Get
     Why." The Washington Post. May 5, 2015. Accessed January 2019. https://www.
     washingtonpost.com/local/millennials-want-a-work-life-balance-their-bosses-
     just-dont-get-why/2015/05/05/1859369e-f376-11e4-84a6-6d7c67c50db0_story.
     html?utm_term=.ab98ac6aa11a.

22   "The Deloitte Millennial Survey 2018." Deloitte. 2018. Accessed January 2019. https://
     www2.deloitte.com/global/en/pages/about-deloitte/articles/millennialsurvey.html.

23   Fry, Richard, and Kim Parker. "Record Shares of Young Adults Have Finished Both
     High School and College." Pew Research Center. November 5, 2012. Accessed 2017.
     http://www.pewsocialtrends.org/2012/11/05/record-shares-of-young-adults-have-
     finished-both-high-school-and-college/.

24   Fry, Richard. "For Millennials, a Bachelor's Degree Continues to Pay Off, but a Master's
     Earns Even More." Pew Research Center. February 28, 2014. Accessed 2017. http://
     www.pewresearch.org/fact-tank/2014/02/28/for-millennials-a-bachelors-degree-
     continues-to-pay-off-but-a-masters-earns-even-more/.

25 "A Look at the Shocking Student Loan Debt Statistics for 2018." Student Loan Hero. May 1, 2018. Accessed 2018. https://studentloanhero.com/student-loan-debt-statistics/.'

26 "Growth of Public Montessori in the United States: 1975-2014." National Center for Montessori in the Public Sector. 2014. Accessed January 2019. https://www.public-montessori.org/white-papers/growth-of-public-montessori-in-the-united-states-1975-2014/.

27 "1.5 Million Homeschooled Students in the United States in 2007." National Center for Education Statistics. December 2008. Accessed January 2019. https://nces.ed.gov/pubs2009/2009030.pdf.

28 Grady, Sarah. "Measuring the Homeschool Population." National Center for Education Statistics. January 4, 2017. Accessed December 2018. https://nces.ed.gov/blogs/nces/post/measuring-the-homeschool-population.

29 Ray, Brian D., PhD. "Homeschooling Growing: Multiple Data Points Show Increase 2012 to 2016 and Later." National Home Education Research Institute. April 20, 2018. Accessed December 2018. https://www.nheri.org/homeschool-population-size-growing/.

30 "CIVIL RIGHTS DATA COLLECTION Data Snapshot: School Discipline." US Department of Education Office for Civil Rights. March 2014. Accessed 2018. https://ocrdata.ed.gov/Downloads/CRDC-School-Discipline-Snapshot.pdf.

31 "Breaking the Link." Charlotte-Mecklenburg Schools. February 2018. Accessed January 2019. http://www.cms.k12.nc.us/cmsdepartments/accountability/Documents/Breaking the Link English.pdf.

32 Kunjufu, Jawanza. *Keeping Black Boys Out of Special Education*. African American Images, 2005.

33 "23 High-Paying Skilled Trades in America." Trade-Schools.net. Accessed December 2018. https://www.trade-schools.net/articles/trade-school-jobs.asp.

34 "Millennial Households Are Poorer than Any Other Generation: Study." Fox Business. September 7, 2017. Accessed 2018. https://www.foxbusiness.com/features/millennial-households-are-poorer-than-any-other-generation-study.

35 Cooper, Betsy, Daniel Cox, Rachel Lienesch, and Robert P. Jones, PhD. "Exodus: Why Americans Are Leaving Religion—and Why They're Unlikely to Come Back." Public Religion Research Institute. September 22, 2016. Accessed December 2018. https://www.prri.org/research/prri-rns-poll-nones-atheist-leaving-religion/.

36 Watson, Misty. "Millennials Are Killing the Church." E-mail interview by author. September 19, 2018.

37 Ter Kuile, Casper. "Millennials Haven't Forgotten Spirituality, They're Just Looking for New Venues." Interview by Judy Woodruff. PBS News Hour. March 3, 2017. Accessed 2017. https://www.pbs.org/newshour/show/millennials-havent-forgotten-spirituality-theyre-just-looking-new-venues.

38 James, S. E., Herman, J. L., Rankin, S., Keisling, M., Mottet, L., & Anafi, M. (2016). The Report of the 2015 US Transgender Survey. Washington, DC: National Center for Transgender Equality

39 National Coalition of Anti-Violence Programs (NCAVP). (2016). Lesbian, Gay, Bisexual, Transgender, Queer, and HIV-Affected Hate Violence in 2016. New York, NY: Emily Waters.

40 "2018 Study on Sexual Harassment and Assault." Stop Street Harassment. February 21, 2018. Accessed December 2018. http://www.stopstreetharassment.org/ resources/2018-national-sexual-abuse-report/.

41 "Sexual Assault and the LGBTQ Community." Human Rights Campaign. 2015. Accessed December 2018. https://www.hrc.org/resources/sexual-assault-and-the-lgbt-community.

42 Twenge, Jean M., Ryne A. Sherman, and Brooke E. Wells. "Sexual Inactivity During Young Adulthood Is More Common Among U.S. Millennials and iGen: Age, Period, and Cohort Effects on Having No Sexual Partners After Age 18."Archives of Sexual Behavior, 2017, Volume 46, Number 2, Page 433

43 "How Does Race Affect the Gender Wage Gap?" American Association of University Women. April 3, 2014. Accessed January 2019. https://www.aauw.org/2014/04/03/ race-and-the-gender-wage-gap/.

44 Gahran, Amy. Stepping Off the Relationship Escalator: Uncommon Love and Life. Off the Escalator Enterprises, 2017.

45 Veaux, Franklin, and Eve Rickert. More Than Two: A Practical Guide to Ethical Polyamory. Thorntree Press, 2014.

46 "U.S. Breastfeeding Rates Continue to Rise." Centers for Disease Control and Prevention. 2013. Accessed 2018. https://www.cdc.gov/media/releases/2013/p0731-breastfeeding-rates.html.

47 Gershoff, Elizabeth T. and Andrew Grogan-Kaylor. "Spanking and child outcomes: Old controversies and new meta-analyses." J Fam Psychol. 2016 Jun; 30(4): 453–469. Published online 2016 Apr 7. doi: 10.1037/fam0000191